C. Barsotti

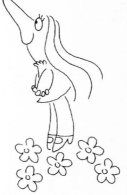

The Essential Charles Barsotti

COMPILED AND EDITED BY LEE LORENZ

WORKMAN PUBLISHING · NEW YORK
A Lee Lorenz Book

For Katie, Ben,
and Jesse
C. B.
For Ava
L.L.

Library of Congress Cataloging-in-Publication Data

Barsotti, C. (Charles)
The Essential Charles Barsotti / compiled and edited by Lee Lorenz.
p.   cm. — (The essential cartoonists library)
ISBN 0-7611-0952-8 (alk. paper)
1. American wit and humor, Pictorial. 2. Barsotti C. (Charles)–
—Interviews. 3. Cartoonists—United States—Interviews.
I. Lorenz, Lee. II. Title. III. Series
NC1429.B29A4 1998
741.5973—dc21   98-51797
CIP

Workman books are available at special discounts when purchased in bulk for premiums and sales promotions as well as for fund-raising or educational use. Special editions can also be created to specification. For
details, contact the Special Sales Director at the address below.

Workman Publishing Company, Inc.
708 Broadway
New York, NY 10003-9555

Printed in the United States

First printing February 1999
10 9 8 7 6 5 4 3 2 1

"It doesn't have a damn thing to do with political correctness, pal.
I'm a sausage and that guy's a wienie."

"Oh, may I freshen your drink, Dr. Marshall?"

PREFACE

Is Charles Barsotti the Zelig of cartooning? His editor at *The Saturday Evening Post,* William Emerson, described him as a supersophisticated yokel when he first arrived in Manhattan from Kansas City. On the other hand, his good friend Bill Porterfield, the writer, claims that Barsotti, though born and raised in Texas, sees the South through the eyes of an outsider. So which is he—a closet slicker in cowboy boots or a good old boy in Topsiders? Perhaps they came together in the famous Friday night hoedowns that he and his wife threw for years at their home in Kansas City. Those evenings combined hot chili, cold beer, and the Texas two-step with high-minded intellectual discussions and poetry readings. The truth is, of course, that Barsotti is, like most of us, a man of contradictions: a cautious, reflective fellow who felt strongly enough about the Vietnam War to stand for Congress in opposition; a sensitive, caring chap who spent seven years running a school for mentally handicapped children and whose drawings have drawn blood from politicians, media hacks, and self-promoters of every stripe. His art is nourished by these contradictions, which are not so much resolved as transcended in his work.

Barsotti's drawings have been a feature of *The New Yorker* since he was hauled aboard by editor William Shawn after *The Saturday Evening Post* sank in 1969. The regular members of Barsotti's long-running *Post* feature "My Kind of People" are now equally familiar to *New Yorker* readers, and they have been joined by an ever-growing cast of characters that allows him to create gags that run from social commentary to simple off-the-wall madness.

A compulsive doodler in his youth, Charley found inspiration in newspaper comic strips and the weekly magazines his parents subscribed to. Since childhood, he has shown himself to be a bit of an outsider. Outsiders abound in his work, and even his familiar King seems to wear his crown uneasily. Role-playing seems to come naturally to him, with no ill side effects. (In someone less gifted, this might be considered a multiple-personality disorder.) To his colleagues, editors, and the public at large, Barsotti is the kind of hardworking citizen every community values. When the national ego threatens to overinflate, however, it is reassuring to know that his alter ego, Superpen, is available to penetrate the bubble with a well-aimed thrust of his Rapidograph.

—Lee Lorenz

CONTENTS

C Barsotti's TEXAS
"I'D KEEP MY EYE ON TEXAS... IT'S BECOMING ONE OF THE MOST IMPORTANT FINANCIAL AND INTELLECTUAL CENTERS OF THE NATION..."
JAMES RESTON, THE NEW YORK TIMES, APRIL 18, 1984
OLE SCOTTY RESTON MUST HAVE BEEN SPYIN' ON ME...
'SPECIALLY THAT INTELLECTUAL PART...
IN FACT THEY OFFERED ME ONE OF THEM NEW CHAIRS AT THE UNIVERSITY...
THEY GOT THESE 32 NEW CHAIRS...
I TOLD 'EM THEY'D HAVE TO MAKE IT A LAZY BOY LOUNGER, BUT THEY SAID NO...
...THEY WAS EDUCATING THE FUTURE SCIENTISTS OF AMERICA.
WELL, I SAID IN THAT CASE THEY SHOULD FORGET THE CHAIRS AND GET 32 BARSTOOLS SO WE COULD BE SURE THEM SUCKERS GOT A HUMANE EDUCATION.
LET ME KNOW IF RESTON WALKS IN. I WANT TO TALK TO HIM ABOUT BEING A FINANCIAL CENTER...
HELL, HE MIGHT BE GOOD FOR SOME VENTURE CAPITAL... OR AT LEAST A ROUND OR TWO.

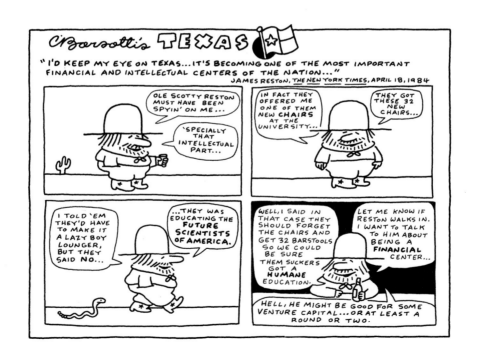

HOME ON THE RANGE

THE TEXAS that Charles Barsotti was born into seems as remote today as the Texas of Sam Houston, Davy Crockett, and the Alamo nearly one century earlier. In 1933 the Texas economy had been devastated by the stock market crash of 1929, and the reforms of Roosevelt's New Deal were just beginning to be felt. Although both his parents recognized and encouraged Charley's artistic talent, it's hardly surprising that they emphasized the importance of sound, reliable, middle-class values: thrift, hard work, and fair play, with the goal of a steady job in one of the professions.

BARSOTTI: I was born September 28, 1933, in San Marcos, Texas. My grandmother lived there. I grew up in San Antonio.

LORENZ: Tell me about your parents.

BARSOTTI: My mom taught school. She had a great name. Dicey (as in a dicey situation) Belle Branum.

LORENZ: She was Irish?

BARSOTTI: Irish and English. Mother's family was Southern. They moved to Texas after the Civil War. My dad was Irish-Italian.

LORENZ: Great mix. What did he do?

BARSOTTI: He was a salesman in a furniture store.

Riding with Gene, Roy, and Hopalong.

LORENZ: Were your parents artistic?

BARSOTTI: No. As far as I know, there weren't any artists in my family.

LORENZ: So whatever it is, it goes way, way back, is that it?

BARSOTTI: Whatever art there is, yes, I suppose it goes back to Florence, Italy. I'd like to claim that, anyway, since that's where the Barsottis are from.

LORENZ: You have a sister.

BARSOTTI: I do. A younger sister, Ann. She's a schoolteacher, already retired, which is really depressing to me.

LORENZ: How much younger?

BARSOTTI: About four years. Ann's a real Texan. On the telephone she sounds like Lady Bird Johnson.

LORENZ: Four years is a pretty good age gap. Were you close to your sister when you were growing up?

BARSOTTI: Not particularly, no. Actually we're closer now. She's sort of the family historian.

LORENZ: How old were you when you moved to San Antonio?

Above: First magazine submission to *Collier's* (age ten). Facing page: First published drawing (high school, age fifteen).

BARSOTTI: I think I was just born in San Marcos, then taken to San Antonio, where my father was working.

LORENZ: So you grew up in the shadows of the Alamo.

BARSOTTI: That's right. In high school, I worked in a Woolworth's right across the street.

LORENZ: Did you live in the city or out in the suburbs?

BARSOTTI: Well it was sort of countrified suburbs. It was a relatively small school district. My mother taught there.

"I'm on the range, but I'm not home on the range."

COWBOY WHO NEVER LEARNED TO HUNKER DOWN

LORENZ: What were your interests in school?

BARSOTTI: Oh, the usual stuff—sandlot ball, going to the movies, hanging out. The only odd thing was that I drew a lot.

LORENZ: When you were in high school, were any of your drawings printed in the school paper?

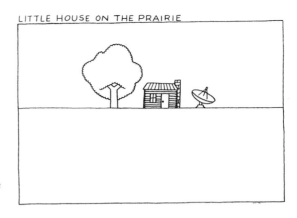

LITTLE HOUSE ON THE PRAIRIE

BARSOTTI: Yes. And in the yearbook, that sort of thing.

LORENZ: When did you become interested in cartooning?

BARSOTTI: That was very early. In San Antonio, when I was growing up, there were essentially three newspapers. One paper had two editions. So we had quite an array of comic strips, and we got all the papers at our house. Dad would bring the Sunday editions home every Saturday night after work. The Sunday comics were a big deal, as I recall.

As a Blue Devil, striking fear in the heart of the opposition.

LORENZ: In an interview, you once mentioned Al Capp as an early influence.

BARSOTTI: Oh, yes, I loved "Li'l Abner."

LORENZ: And who else?

BARSOTTI: My goodness, let's see. Oh, everybody else. You know, I just read 'em all. "Blondie," "Prince Valiant," "Jiggs and Maggie." In fact, my dog was named Jiggs.

COLLEGE DAYS

By the time he was creating cartoons for his high school paper, Charley had turned his attention from the comic strips to the more challenging world of the single-panel magazine gag cartoons. *The Saturday Evening Post,* which later played a decisive role in his career, was welcomed weekly into the Barsotti household, as were two other publications that featured cartoons, *Look* and *Collier's*. His first encounter with the comic masters of *The New Yorker* didn't occur until he was already in college, but it was, in his own words, decisive: "Richter, Addams, Price, Darrow, Cobean, their work was a revelation to me. They were funny, and they could draw. And, of

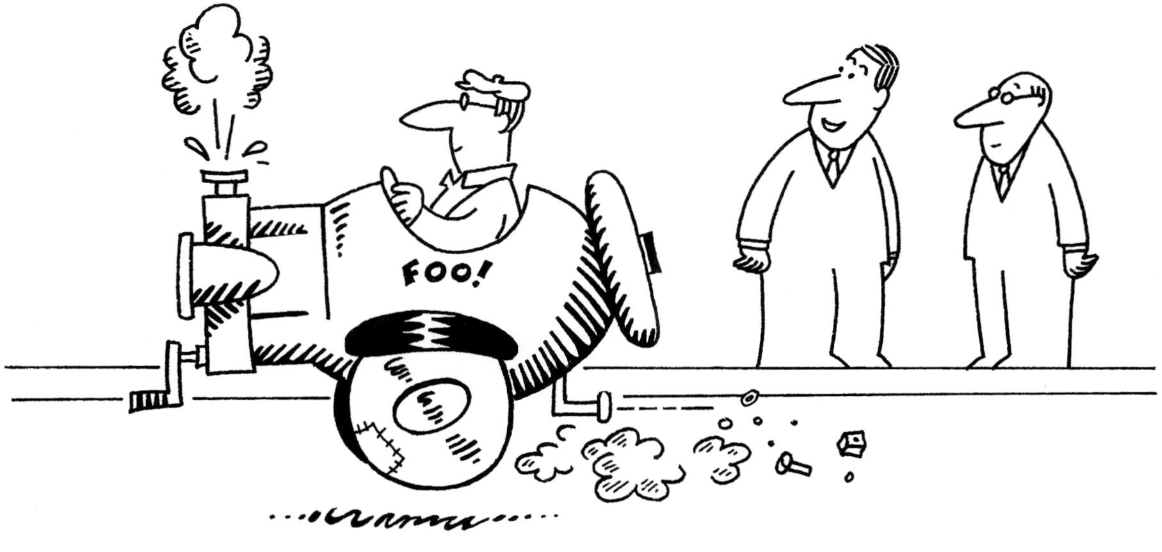
FOO!

"Wow, you just don't see a restoration job like that every day."

The strips of Charley's childhood left indelible impressions. At left, an homage to "Smokey Stover"; above, a nod to "Buck Rogers."

course, I knew they were sophisticated because they were from New York." Long before he graduated, Charley announced his determination to draw for *The New Yorker*. Many who knew him were skeptical, but those who knew him well never doubted for a minute that he'd pull it off.

LORENZ: You picked a college in your own home state?

BARSOTTI: Yes. In fact, I came full circle. Southwest Texas State was back in San Marcos.

LORENZ: Your yearbook said you graduated with a degree in social science.

BARSOTTI: Is that what it says? I'll take it.

LORENZ: What is social science?

BARSOTTI: Beats the hell out of me. I took a lot of history and stuff like that.

LORENZ: So at that point you hadn't really decided you wanted to pursue a career in cartooning. Or had you?

THOUGHTS FROM BARSOTTI

College in the fifties was a conformist type of situation. There wasn't much student protest at the time, except maybe against the food in the cafeteria. I suppose the conformity was something of a burden. I wrote cartoons for the college Star, *and it was a great experience. You sure got an immediate reaction. I recommend it for everyone.*

The work I did for the Star *was pretty heavily censored. Just to be sure I didn't do anything too racy or talk about beer too much or girls too much or anything like that, Dr. Flowers, the president, used to go over my work. He wasn't averse to pasting little bits of white paper on the cartoons to edit out whatever he found offensive.*

The head of our English department was fired because he wrote something satirical about Texas politics. When that happened, I had a heck of a time getting my thoughts about it in the paper, so I had to do it by means of cartoon puns that somehow got through. The art department really tried to discourage me from cartooning. They thought it inhibited me somehow. So I could never really get serious about the art department. I just wanted to cartoon.

BARSOTTI: I guess I'm essentially a slow starter. I knew I wanted to, but I didn't know if I'd be able to. I did know I'd have to get a job right away.

LORENZ: So what you studied in college was sort of your backup system.

BARSOTTI: Something like that. But first I went into the army.

LORENZ: You were drafted.

BARSOTTI: That's right. I ended up serving in San Antonio at Fort Sam Houston. I was a company clerk. It was a big, strange medical outfit . . .

LORENZ: So you didn't have to shoot anybody.

BARSOTTI: No. Thank goodness.

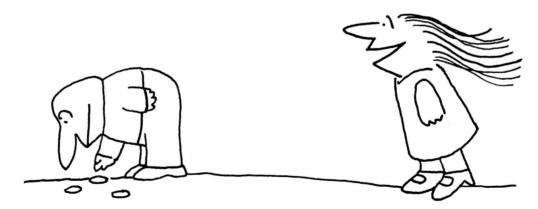

"Has it occurred to you, Murray, that you may find more in these lonely hills than flat stones to skip across the pond?"

PORTRAIT OF AN ARTIST WITH A YOUNG FAMILY

LORENZ: You married young, didn't you? And then you went from the altar to the army.

BARSOTTI: Well, I got married in 1955 and we started a family pretty early.

LORENZ: This was to Jo Ann. She was your college sweetheart, right? What did she study when you were in school together?

BARSOTTI: Music. She was a very talented singer. She also played the piano, but her real gift was singing.

LORENZ: And you had four children together.

"I'd like to remind you again, Winfield, that daydreaming is only a <u>part</u> of the creative process."

BARSOTTI: Yes, Kerry, Wendy, Sue, and Mike. And later, after Ramoth and I were married, I adopted her daughter, Jean.

LORENZ: Do any of them have musical or artistic talent?

BARSOTTI: Each is a bundle of talent.

LORENZ: How many grandchildren do you have?

BARSOTTI: Three. Katie, Ben, and Jesse—a handsome lot and wildly talented, of course.

"Excuse me, sir, but I'm on a working vacation. Would you like to buy a tie?"

*"That's wonderful, Curtis. I, too, think a hot, balanced breakfast
is the best preparation for the day ahead."*

LORENZ: After your discharge, you became an administrator at a school for mentally challenged kids. A long way from cartooning.

BARSOTTI: Well, I had been working at the school as an undergraduate. I was able to teach crafts. I was a lifeguard, and I even got to teach children with Down's syndrome how to swim.

LORENZ: Tell me about the school.

BARSOTTI: It was a residential treatment center, which meant the patients actually lived there.

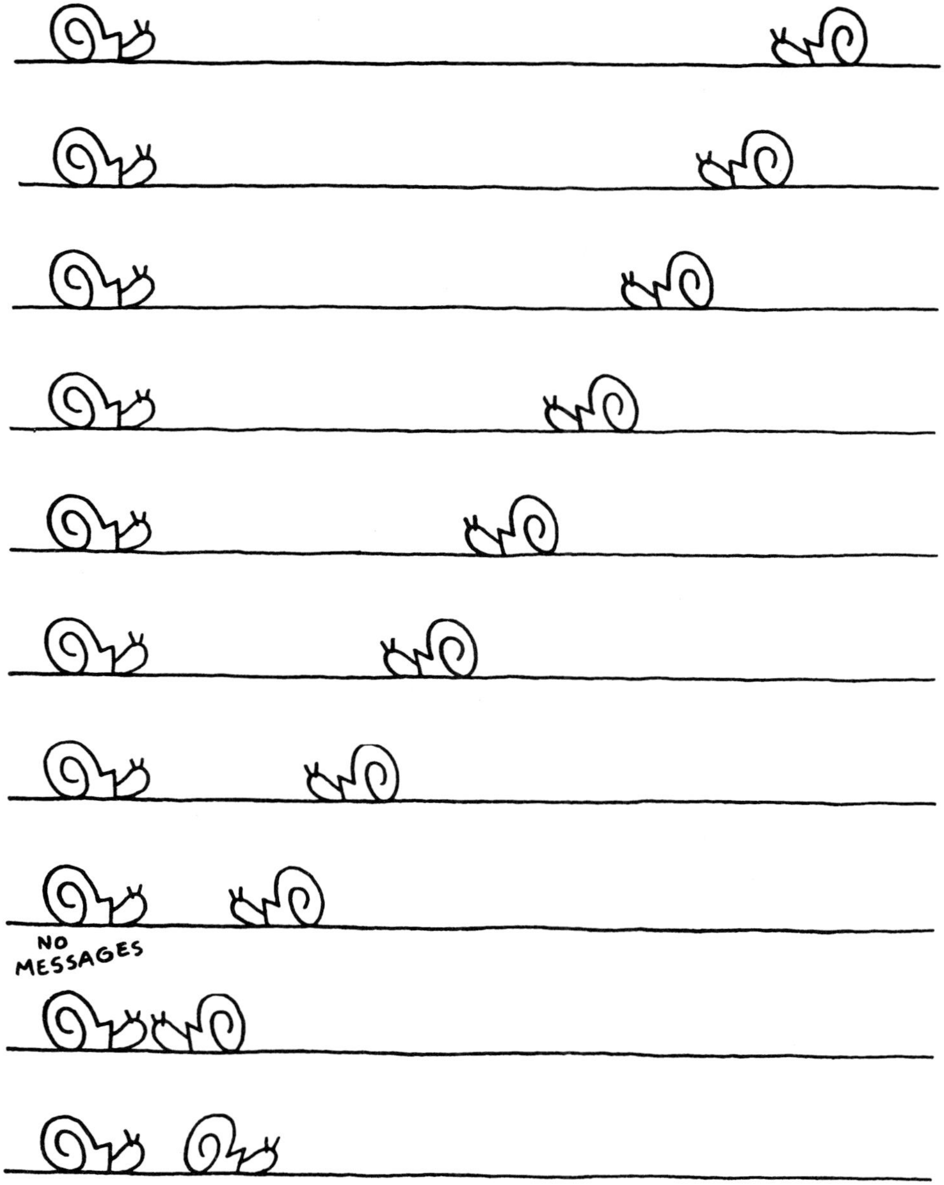
NO MESSAGES

LORENZ: So you started there as a teacher and became an administrator.

BARSOTTI: Actually, I started as a counselor. Then I went back as a teacher after the army, and something happened real quickly—the owners of the school came in and said they'd like me to run the place.

LORENZ: Being married with kids, this was a good steady job to have.

BARSOTTI: Well, it was a good job, but it was hard work, too.

LORENZ: And you were trying to pursue cartooning in some way at that point.

BARSOTTI: Yes, I was. At first I thought I'd go back and get a master's degree in education, but I became very disenchanted with that. I was then absolutely consumed by the school and the responsibilities there. So I never pursued an advanced degree.

LORENZ: But you were submitting cartoons here and there through the mail?

BARSOTTI: I was a little. I still had the idea of a comic strip. I thought it was a good thing to do, and I was hacking around with that.

LORENZ: Do you remember some of the ideas you had for strips back then?

BARSOTTI: Yes, but I'd rather forget them.

LORENZ: Were they adventure strips or gag strips?

BARSOTTI: Gag strips.

LORENZ: Did any of the characters that you later developed appear in those strips? A dog or a king? Or Emma June?

BARSOTTI: No dogs, no kings. Nothing I can particularly think of. And I did stuff locally, you know. It was a small university town. I did ads for a laundry —in fact, they're still using my trademark.

A BITE OF THE APPLE

LORENZ: What was the turning point? I mean, there you were, working in a small Texas town, then suddenly you're selling stuff to nationwide magazines.

BARSOTTI: The residential schools were private. I ran a couple of them, and the president of the schools, Lyndon Brown, and I were good friends. He had a wide range of interests—he was a big theater buff, for example. And he was very interested in my cartooning. He was getting ready for a business trip to New York, and he called and said, "Why don't you take the afternoon off, go home and draw some stuff, and come to New York with me?" I told him I couldn't afford the trip, but he offered to cover the expenses. He said I could pay it back from whatever I made from the trip.

LORENZ: How did you do?

BARSOTTI: Better than I should have. I paid him back and made a few bucks extra. I hadn't made any appointments in advance—I just went down to the hotel lobby and checked the phone book. I went to *Esquire,* but they weren't very receptive. Most magazines at least let me drop things off. I sold an idea to *The New Yorker* out of the batch I left there. Walking down the street, I noticed a plaque on a building that said PAGEANT MAGAZINE, so I stopped in there. They were real encouraging and bought some stuff on the spot.

LORENZ: So the trip paid for itself.

BARSOTTI: More than that. It really made me feel I could market my stuff.

LORENZ: It makes all the difference when somebody asks you to do it, doesn't it? What was that fellow's name?

BARSOTTI: Lyndon Brown. He was very conservative politically, he was from central Texas, and his name was Lyndon. He just hated Lyndon Johnson. Of course, a lot of people down there did.

LORENZ: Well, he must have taken a lot of pride later on in the fact that eventually you had quite a career as a cartoonist.

BARSOTTI: Yes, he did. Several years back I was in Dallas, covering the 1984 G.O.P. convention for *USA Today.* He had been ill, and he had reestablished contact with us so we planned to go on to Austin, where he lived. As soon as the convention was over, we drove down to meet him for dinner that night. We were all looking forward to this. But then he died, so instead of going to dinner with him, we went to his funeral.

But, yeah, he was very proud that he helped me get started. As a matter of fact, I think he had the original of the very first cartoon I had in *The New Yorker.*

Barsotti's first *New Yorker* cartoon, August 25, 1962.

*"Just think!
If it weren't for nuclear fission,
we might never have met!"*

PAGEANT

**YOU'VE BEEN
A BRICK THROUGH
IT ALL**

*Some people
just don't
know their
place*

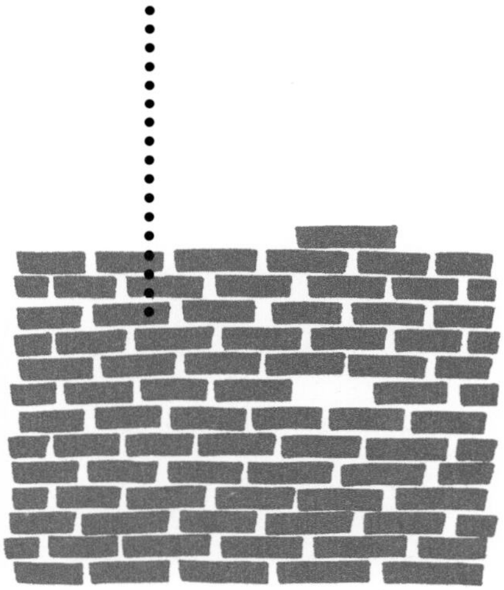

*Head to foot . . .
Head to foot . . .
Who's to know?*

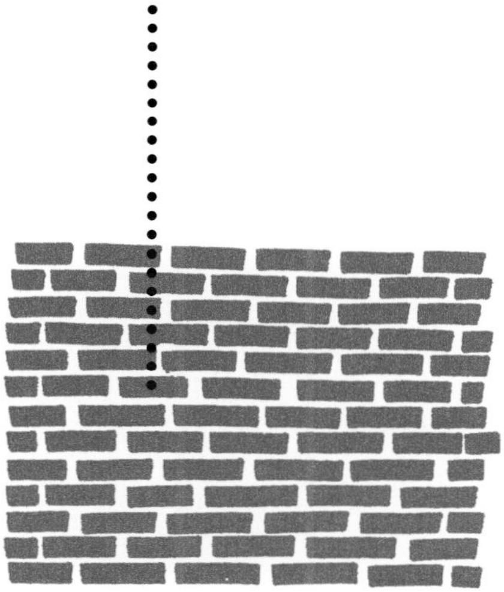

*Here comes the
cavalry at last!*

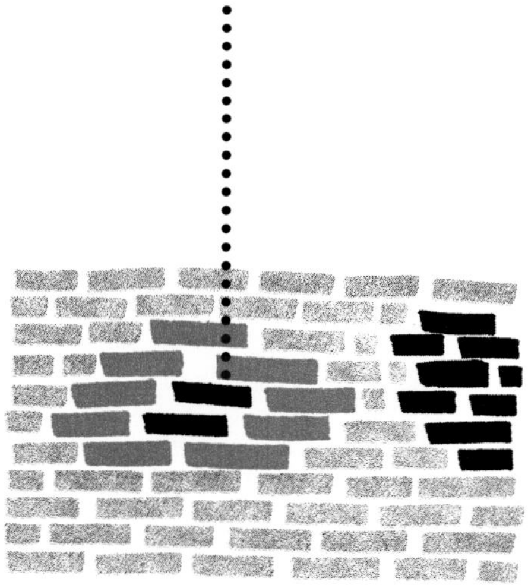

Dr. Livingstone, I presume

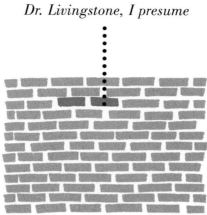

Try to relax

*You've got to pull
yourself together*

*Maybe you just
weren't cut out to
be a brick*

FIGURE 1

FIGURE 2

ALERT MEMBER IN OFFICIAL
ATTIRE COMMANDS RESPECT

In these perilous times every American must ask himself: "What have I done for the protection of my country today?"

It is to answer just such a question that the editors of PAGEANT have decided to print the following excerpts from the Alert Defense pamphlet, *A Manual for Dirigible Watchers,* as a Public Service.

The backbone of this country's dirigible protection team is an alert group of selfless citizens who have

FIGURE 3

organized under the banner of the Civilian Watchers for Unidentified Dirigibles, or CWUD.

The vast membership of CWUD volunteered largely because of the excellent posters designed to recruit a vast membership (**see Figure 1**).

Upon gaining membership the Public Spirited Citizen is then outfitted in a snappy uniform (**see Figure 2**). The individual is then allowed to wear the coveted membership pin (**see Figure 3**) in his lapel.

A DIRIGIBLE

FIGURE 4

A   B

HOW TO SEARCH FOR UNIDENTIFIED DIRIGIBLES

A) LOOK UP
B) UP

FIGURE 5

The purpose of dirigible watching is to watch for dirigibles; ergo, one must be able to identify a dirigible. If you see an object in the sky that looks a great deal like a big, fat floating cigar it is in all likelihood a dirigible, unless, of course, it turns out to be a big, fat floating cigar.

We digress. To aid you in your search for dirigibles, we have prepared the following diagram (see **Figure 4**).

Now that you know what a dirigible looks like, you must learn how to look for a dirigible. The Proper Method is demonstrated in Figure 5 (see **Figure 5**).

The Improper Method for looking for dirigibles is diagramed in Figure 6 (see **Figure 6**).

It should be noted that there is an auxiliary organization for those who are unable to devote full time to dirigible watching. These citizens are called Free Lance Dirigible Watchers.

AN IMPROPER WAY TO SEARCH FOR DIRIGIBLES

FIGURE 6

UPON SIGHTING A DIRIGIBLE NOTIFY YOUR FELLOWS THUSLY:

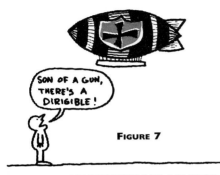

FIGURE 7

THE <u>WRONG</u> THING TO SAY UPON SIGHTING A DIRIGIBLE:

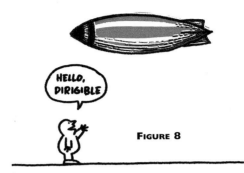

FIGURE 8

THAT IS THE CORRECT THING TO SAY UPON SIGHTING A DIRIGIBLE

FIGURE 9

A) Approved dirigible fall-out shelter.

B) Also approved dirigible fall-out shelter.

C) Or anything else because you never know what might fall out of a dirigible.

There has been some criticism of the CWUD program because of the apparent lack of a Distant Early Warning system. This simply is not true. Our Distant Early Warning system is directly overhead which is jolly well soon enough for dirigibles.

When one sights a dirigible one must notify one's fellows by shouting the following: "SON OF A GUN, THERE IS A DIRIGIBLE!" (see **Figure 8**). Do not use casual salutations (see **Figure 8**).

Approved dirigible shelters are available in virtually every community in the country (see **Figure 9**), and while we are not absolutely sure they will prevent a dirigible from doing whatever it is that dirigibles do, we feel that even if they do do it, it will make a great conversation opener the next time you are ill at ease in an articulate, erudite group.

DIRIGIBLES ARE SOMETIMES CLEVERLY DISGUISED

FIGURE 10

AND SOMETIMES NOT

FIGURE 11

As you advance in skill as a dirigible watcher you must acquaint yourself with the tricks of the dirigible trade. Figures 10 and 11 (see **Figures 10 and 11**) will prepare you for the worst.

Now that you have had your basic training in dirigible watching let us urge you to go out into your communities, to your schools, to your factories, to your offices, and watch for dirigibles (see **Figures 12 and 13**).

But mostly go outdoors.

IT IS NOW TIME TO PUT OUR TRAINING BEHIND US AND MARCH FORTH TO OUR FACTORIES, SCHOOLS, AND OFFICES! HOWEVER . . .

FIGURE 12

OFTEN THE FOLLOWING OBJECTS ARE REPORTED AS DIRIGIBLES BY OUR ALERT MEMBERS IN:

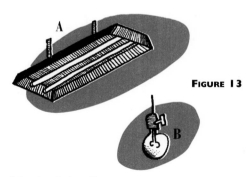

FIGURE 13

A) Factories, schools, or offices

B) Old factories, schools, or offices

(Usually, these reports are not extremely reliable; however, one cannot be too careful)

*"Congratulations. You have the skills we're looking for,
and you'll just fit a cubicle."*

OUT OF THE NEST

EVERYONE REMEMBERS where he was when Kennedy was shot. On November 22, 1963, Charles Barsotti was sitting in his office at a school for mentally challenged children, mulling over the future. A few months earlier, he had replied to a blind ad in *Advertising Age* and received an encouraging response along with a package of application forms. It still lay in his bottom drawer, unanswered. A position with Hallmark would bring him closer to his ambition to become a cartoonist. On the other hand, it would mean moving with his school-age children to Kansas City. The Kennedy assassination cast the situation in a whole new light.

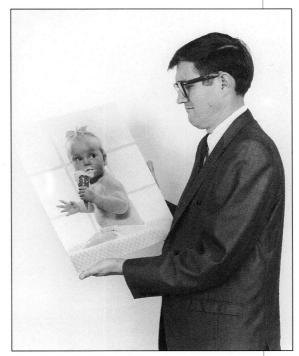

Test run for an early promotional photo at Hallmark.

BARSOTTI: That evening I drove around San Marcos, trying to sort out my thoughts. (It seems to me that in those days we Texans did a lot of driving around to sort ourselves out.) I drove by the high school football stadium, and the game was in a full roar. It didn't seem right—not that much did. It was probably time to leave.

HALLMARK GREETINGS

The questionnaire from Hallmark included a psychological profile. With some guidance from William White's *The Organization Man*, Barsotti filled it out and shipped the whole bundle off to Hallmark. In 1964 he packed his wife and four kids into the car and took off for Kansas City. He reported for his new job in yet one more of his many disguises—the corporate man. Fortunately, his new boss, Robert McCluskey, saw through the charcoal gray suit and black tie to the free spirit within. Charley was assigned to the newly created Contemporary Design department—the Hallmark equivalent of Warner Brothers' Animation Division, "The Skunk Works." "Our orders were to create cards that looked different from the regular line," recalls McCluskey. "As long as we were successful, they left us alone to do what we wanted." In fact, the line was hugely successful.

Although Charley did more writing than drawing, he still considers his four years at Hallmark an indispensable part of his development as a cartoonist. Another Hallmark colleague, Gordon MacKenzie, remembers Barsotti as a vivid presence: "He brought a freedom that was just wonderful, and he was amazingly prolific. He'd bring in stacks of cartoons he was submitting to the *Post* and show them around. He called what he was doing 'Frecklebelly,' it was so innocent and so silly and so honest."

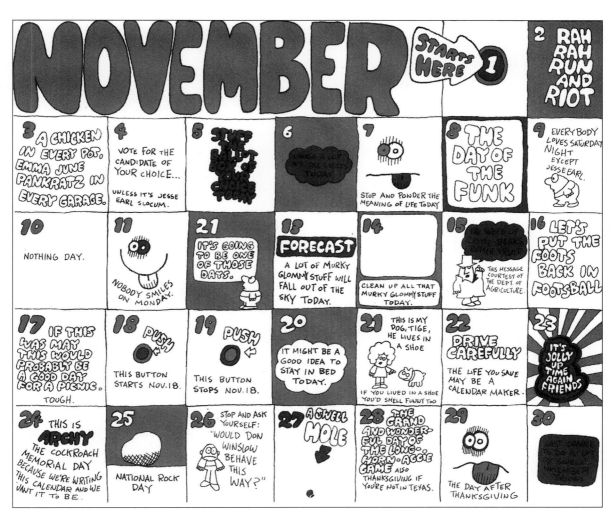

Hallmark's sixteen-month "Ralph" calendar was a cooperative enterprise to which Charley contributed both drawings and ideas. When November rolled around, he gave everyone else a well-deserved breather and tackled it singlehandedly.

LORENZ: I understand you had a brush with one of *The New Yorker*'s greats while you were at Hallmark.

BARSOTTI: Yes, I illustrated a booklet of humorous verse by Ogden Nash. A colleague, Bill Peterson, was the art director, and with Bill's encouragement (and a set of the then-new Rapidograph pens) I changed my style of drawing. So, yes, my brush with Ogden Nash was very important to me.

A 1977 Hallmark Engagement Calendar

LORENZ: You were still working at Hallmark when your first big break came. Tell me about that.

BARSOTTI: That was in 1966. Mostly I did ideas and some editing at Hallmark, but I was working on my own. Every weekend I did a batch of cartoons and sent them off to magazines like *Look, The Saturday Evening Post,* and, of course, *The New Yorker.* The *Post* had bought a few things, and then one day something really weird happened. With my Rapidograph pens, I just went wild. I had been working with regular straight pens, and of course you have to stop and dip all the time. With the Rapidographs, you never have to stop— and I didn't. I got so excited, I whipped up two large batches and shipped them off to the *Post.*

Barsotti's association with "Sally Bananas" has been as durable as William Steig's association with "Small Fry." Charley was well established at *The New Yorker* in the mid-seventies when Hallmark invited him to reprise his proto-feminist heroine in an engagement calendar. As his selections make clear, the years diminished neither her skepticism nor her resiliency.

LORENZ: Then what happened?

BARSOTTI: At first, nothing. Then, two weeks later, I got a phone call from some guy with a heavy New York accent who said he was Mike Mooney from the *Post*. Now, I knew Mooney was a Princeton man, and I had just heard another Princeton man, the social anthropologist Ashley Montagu, give a lecture. This guy on the phone sure didn't sound like a Princeton man. He was telling me how much he loved my stuff and how he had it taped up all over the office. He called it the "museum of Barsotti." I thought it was a joke—and not a very funny one—but after ten minutes of this I realized he wasn't kidding. He convinced the editor, William Emerson, to feature my stuff. I started with a three-page spread and then a biweekly panel called "My Kind of People."

EASTWARD HO!

BARSOTTI: I got on with Emerson quite well, and in 1966 he asked me to come east and be the *Post*'s cartoon editor.

LORENZ: What was it like moving to the east coast?

BARSOTTI: I loved it. We rented a comfortable house in Mamaroneck—just thirty minutes from Manhattan. It was a great little neighborhood. Soon after we moved in, a water main burst right down the block. It was a Sunday afternoon. First the kids came out in their bathing suits. Then the parents started gathering. Pretty soon drinks were being passed around, and by sundown a neighborhood barbecue was in full swing. Real Easterners love to complain about commuting, but I thought it was great—a quiet half-hour on the train with *The New York Times* and a third cup of coffee.

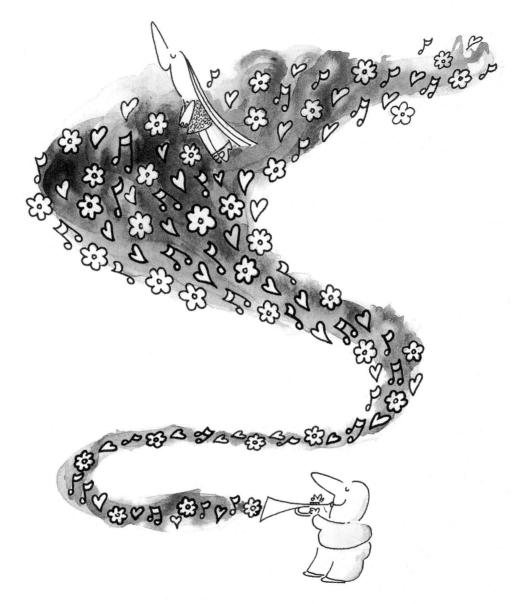

"Oh, Harry, <u>nobody</u> plays 'The Stars and Stripes Forever' the way you do."

the professionals

by *CBarsotti*

"Just take my word for it, lady. This is to plumbing what the Mona Lisa is to art."

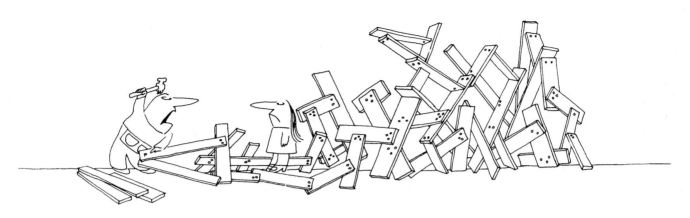

"I'm a carpenter, ma'am;
you want anything particular built, you call an architect."

"If you will recall, sir, I only said I was
a tailor. I never said I was a good tailor."

"Are we to assume, then, Madame,
that you are some sort of anarchist?"

"*Actually, I pictured a much younger man.*"

THE OTHER SIDE
OF THE DESK

Every cartoonist feels that his or her best work is routinely passed over by editors. Ideally, they would all like to edit their own work. Charley Barsotti is one of the few artists (Sam Gross and myself are two others) who have had the opportunity to experience the field from the editor's perspective.

LORENZ: How did you feel about trading your cartoonist's rags for the royal regalia of editor?

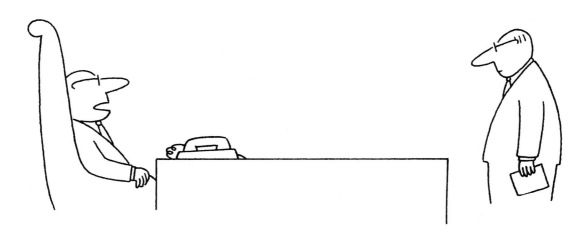

"Send Williamson a signal. Tell him he's fired."

BARSOTTI: I loved it. William Emerson was terrific to work with, although we had a few disagreements. Every once in a while, he'd remind me that he was the "goddamned editor."

LORENZ: You also got to work with other cartoonists.

BARSOTTI: That was the best part. I really love cartooning, and I thought the magazine didn't pay cartoonists enough attention. I arranged lunches with Emerson and the artists, and occasionally I would take a bunch of them out to lunch as a kind of "thank you." It was a treat to publish work by cartoonists I thought had been overlooked. I published some talented guys from Hallmark, Dean Vietor, and Bruce Cochran.

"Just a few more pages, Hansen, and we'll take a short break."

LORENZ: In fact, you were the first to print George Booth.

BARSOTTI: Yes, that was a big thrill. He came in one afternoon and said that he and his wife, Dione, had been looking at my stuff and thought maybe I'd understand *his* stuff. He spread some cartoons out on my desk, and having a keen editorial eye—and not being a damn fool—I knew in an instant that George was special. We published one or two right away, and Emerson agreed to run a multipage spread of Booth's work. The idea was to run a spread of cartoons, not on a theme as was usual but to properly introduce George to the *Post* readers.

LORENZ: I don't remember seeing that.

BARSOTTI: It never ran. In January of 1969, the *Post* folded. In addition to losing the Booth spread, I also missed the chance to publish my first *Post* cover, slated for the next issue. The last I saw of it, Emerson was holding it up for the TV cameras during the post-mortem interviews.

I went into the *Post* offices three days a week. Wednesday I met with the artists, Thursday I went over the cartoons, and Friday Emerson and I had the art meeting. At some magazines, the art meeting includes the entire

The original art for Charley's never-published *Post* cover seems to have gone down with the ship. The xerox reproduced above is his only remaining souvenir.

editorial board. Emerson felt strongly that it should be limited to the two of us. His thinking was based on his experience as a reporter covering beauty contests down South. He said there were always five judges and the second-prettiest girl always won. With just two, he felt we had a better chance of buying the unique and the best.

The big advantage of having the art meeting late on Fridays was that afterward we could ride out to Westchester in the bar car and unwind. I always told Emerson that the only way they'd get me out of the *Post* was to carry me out. After it folded, we all had so much to drink that they did.

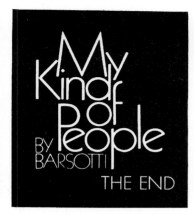

My Kind of People

BY BARSOTTI

THE END

PEACE

"Deal."

"Operator, I love you."

"Don't they know this neighborhood is zoned?"

"Oh damn."

"You'd think something as important as this they'd broadcast in color."

"But yesterday you were only asking a dollar ninety-five."

"But what could I have done?"

EMMA JUNE

One of the most memorable performers in Barsotti's *Post* feature "My Kind of People" was an irrepressible young woman he named Emma June. Romantic yet clear-eyed, ambitious but independent, she both personified and transcended feminism. In fact, any "ism" was foreign to her nature, with the possible exception of individualism.

"Let me see if I have this straight, Miss. He should be tall, but not too tall, liberal but not too liberal..."

"...to the animal that is _me_?!!"

When the Post sank, Barsotti expanded a handful of these magazine appearances into a droll and delightful fairy tale, published as *A Girl Needs a Little Action.* In this version, the fairy godmother role is assumed by a wise-cracking, overworked Lucky Star. Although her go-for-it approach to life was revived in Barsotti's long-running strip called "Sally Bananas" and still echoes in his cartoon chronicles of the gender wars, Emma June remains a splendid achievement in her own right.

"I *know* it's the Men's Bar, that's why I'm here."

"But, Mister Bonfigli, you have an advantage... being Italian and all."

"Gee, you sure know how to pack a picnic basket."

"That's not _our_ song!!"

"Wait right here.
I'll get my toothbrush!"

"...so if there's
ever anything
we can do for
you..."

CARTOONING IN THE SIXTIES

Charley Barsotti's work began appearing in national magazines during a period of great social upheaval, the sixties. The civil rights movement, the divisive conflict in Vietnam, and the emergence of the hippie counterculture combined to raise the country's social conscience. This was reflected at all levels of popular culture, and even such tradition-bound publications as *The Saturday Evening Post* were affected. Cartooning as a form of social commentary, long the exclusive province of *The New Yorker,* began appearing regularly in magazines such as *Esquire, Look,* the newly hatched *Playboy,* and especially *The Saturday Evening Post.*

"If consumption hadn't got the late Mr. Deffendorf, you can rest assured the rise of the New Left would have."

"Wait. I've come to your planet in peace."

The *Post* cartoon editor, Mike Mooney, was vocally pro-civil rights and antiwar, and his views were increasingly reflected in the magazine's cartoons, especially in a newly created feature entitled "America, America." *The New Yorker*'s reluctance to echo in its cartoons the strong antiwar views expressed weekly in "Notes and Comments" by Jonathan Schell allowed the *Post* to assume the lead in publishing contemporary social comment. These liberal views strongly reflected Barsotti's own, and when he assumed the position of cartoon editor in 1968, the magazine's political edge became even sharper.

America, America

"Move along, Bud, this neighborhood isn't zoned for poetry."

"You need a haircut."

"Steak tartare."

"Well, for one thing, the other Cary Grant has a better tailor."

EMMA JUNE

*"You're a safe date, Monroe.
A thirty-three-year-old safe date!"*

"I gave at the office."

END OF AN ERA

The editorial freedom enjoyed by magazine cartoonists in the sixties served to mask less happy developments in the industry. The shift of advertising dollars from magazines to television was accelerating, and though circulations remained steady, or in some cases actually grew, profits continued to fall. (Success in publishing is measured in terms of advertising dollars, not subscription lists. When *The Saturday Evening Post* folded, it had the largest readership in its history.) In an effort to turn the tide, magazines began to "reinvent" themselves. It was surely no coincidence that the ascendance of the art director dates from this period. Most cartoonists were only vaguely aware that magazines even had art directors, until, as more and more magazines began repackaging themselves, they began to be pressed further and further into the margins.

"Miss Wexler, what are the prevailing winds?"

A magazine's look became more important than its editorial content. It should be simple, bold, and, above all, predictable. Among the elements an art director works with—typography, photography, layout—the least predictable is cartoons. Styles vary, and they don't come in uniform shapes. Some insinuate themselves into the reader's consciousness, and some explode off the page. Cartoonists and art directors, it developed, are natural enemies, and it soon became apparent which side had the firepower. Redesign projects at *Esquire* and *Sports Illustrated* eliminated cartoons altogether. Clay Felker's original proposal for *New York* magazine included cartoons, only to have them banished at the last moment by his all-powerful art director, the designer Milton Glazer.

"It's always poor you, isn't it, Albert?"

"Good, we're all agreed. I like it when we're all agreed."

"The meeting will come to order."

A REALIZATION

As the sixties guttered out, it became clear that the era of the general-interest, national-circulation weekly was dying with it. *Collier's* folded, then *The Saturday Evening Post,* and finally *Look.* The *Saturday Review* died and was buried, then dug up again, and finally laid to rest for good. Some of the more resourceful magazine cartoonists managed to survive and even prosper in the world of newspaper comic strips. Johnny Hart created "B.C.," Charley Schulz created "Peanuts," and of course Mort Walker created an entire cartoon dynasty that included "Beetle Bailey" and "Hi and Lois." And there were a lucky few, like Charles Barsotti and George Booth, who managed to be pulled from the sea by *The New Yorker* magazine.

LIFE AFTER THE POST

LORENZ: Losing the *Post* must have been a terrible blow. What happened next?

BARSOTTI: At the time of the *Post's* collapse, William Shawn called Emerson and asked him if there was anything he could do. Emerson, God bless him, said, "See Booth and Barsotti."

So the next Friday I was ushered into Shawn's office. I can't remember what he said, but as bad as I felt, I came out feeling like a million dollars. Shawn said I should meet with Jim Geraghty, *The New Yorker's* art editor. The next week I had lunch with Geraghty and the cartoonist Frank Modell, who was working as Geraghty's assistant. It was a very pleasant lunch, very funny thanks to Frank, and very vague. Way too vague. So while I continued to submit cartoons to *The New Yorker,* I was also working on a comic strip,

"Go! Go! Go! Go!"

"SALLY BANANAS"

"SALLY BANANAS"

"SALLY BANANAS"

"SALLY BANANAS"

"Sally Bananas," for the Newsday syndicate. I had no idea that I would be getting a *New Yorker* contract the following December, or I might well have chucked—or at least held off on—the comic strip. The strip was launched in October, and in December I was given a *New Yorker* contract.

LORENZ: You also published a book based on your *Post* character Emma June about the same time.

BARSOTTI: Yes, it all happened about the same time. I was hustling around. I had kids who needed Big Wheels and Barbies. And I was in shock. Keep in mind, *The Saturday Evening Post* was a national institution that I had grown up with—it wasn't supposed to go belly up. But I remember that summer sitting at the neighborhood pool and thinking, "My God, maybe we're going to make it after all."

BROADSIDES

WE MUST HOLD TO OUR IDEALS!...

12/12

...IF WE CAN REMEMBER THEM.

LIFE'S A GAME ALL RIGHT...

12/13

...AND I'VE USED UP ALL MY TIME OUTS

IF I'M MIDDLE CLASS AND MIDDLE AGED...

12/14

...WHY AM I ON EDGE ALL THE TIME?

ON THE HIGHWAY OF LIFE...

12/15

...I'M A DETOUR.

I USED TO LET A SMILE BE MY UMBRELLA...

...BUT MY FACE MILDEWED.

12/16

SOME DAYS I FEEL LIKE AN ELBOW...

12/17

...IN THE BUTTER DISH OF LIFE.

Above and opposite: two very different incarnations of Barsotti's "everyman."

56

P.J. McFEY
MANAGEMENT BROUGHT IN A MOTIVATIONAL SPEAKER TO FIRE US UP. THE GUY SAID WE SHOULD BELIEVE IN OURSELVES AND REACH FOR GREATNESS.
HALF THE STAFF WENT OVER TO THE COMPETITION.
THIS IS ONE OF THOSE MORNINGS~ I JUST CAN'T GET MYSELF GOING...
BUS STOP
BOOM!
THANKS, BUT SOME MORNINGS EVEN A JUMP START WON'T HELP.
EUREKA!
WE DID IT!
CREATIVE DEPT.
THEY PROBABLY FIGURED OUT A WAY TO EXTRACT THE ALCOHOL FROM THEIR DRAWING INK.

PLAYBOY

In retrospect, Charley was only half right. His professional life was booming, but the unexpected and stressful shifts in his career had taken a heavy toll on his marriage. In 1973, he and Jo Ann divorced. At about the same time, he added *Playboy* to his list of clients.

LORENZ: Your *Playboy* drawings exude a sense of, shall I say, playfulness. Did you enjoy working for them?

BARSOTTI: Absolutely, I surely did and do. I first sold them some nonsexy cartoons, and then Michelle Urry, the cartoon editor, wrote and said, in essence, "Come on and give it a shot." Yes, I've really enjoyed it.

"An honest man? No, I'm looking to get laid."

"Why, Clarice, you didn't tell me your young gentleman juggled fish."

LORENZ: I understand your *Playboy* work once generated more excitement than you bargained for.

BARSOTTI: Oh, man! That was when I moved back to Kansas City. I was getting a divorce. I was broke and practically living in my car. But things can always get worse. All of a sudden, some bozo with a badge shows up and drops a subpoena on me! I had done a drawing for *Playboy* of a guy with a babe in what you might call a compromising position. The hostess interrupts them to pass the hors d'oeuvres. I made up a name for the guy, and just to be on the safe side I checked it against the Kansas City phone book. It wasn't listed, so I thought it was okay. I should have checked the London phone book. It turned out to be the name of some titled, wealthy Englishman—Lord something or other. He was not, as the English say, amused.

"I'm here to spread the good word, brother."

LORENZ: Well, I don't see any jail time on your resumé, so I guess it blew over, so to speak.

BARSOTTI: They were amazingly decent about it. *Playboy* settled out of court and spared me the details. Michelle Urry went to bat for me, and she still buys my stuff. A great woman.

"You the asshole who ordered blackened redfish?"

"I suppose we can take comfort in the fact that the experts don't know what's going on either."

AT THE NEW YORKER

I N 1970, when Barsotti signed his first contract with *The New Yorker*, the art of the magazine was dominated by contributors who hailed back to the thirties. Arno had recently died, but George Price, Charles Addams, and Whitney Darrow, Jr., were still going strong. Although Saul Steinberg and William Steig were contributing innovative work, the recognized *"New Yorker* style" was deeply rooted in the traditional, more illustrative work of those early masters. The most influential cartoonist of the moment was the late Charles Saxon. Though very contemporary in tone, Saxon's solid draftsmanship and masterful composition clearly celebrated the great comic artists of the past.

Barsotti's first contributions to *The New Yorker* contrasted refreshingly with this tradition. His simple line drawings evoked the early work of Otto Soglow and James Thurber and anticipated the more personal stylists to come, like Jack Zeigler and Roz Chast. While more tradition-bound artists like Handelsman, Reilly, Weber, and myself competed for space in the magazine, free spirits like Ed Koren and Charles Barsotti quietly created a niche for their more innovative comic styles.

62

"I'll leave, Margaret, but I won't get lost."

"I consider myself a passionate man, but, of course, a lawyer first."

"*Pretty good,
but I'll bet you can't hit him again.*"

"*I plead guilty, Your Honor, but only in a nice, white-collar sort of way.*"

POWER AND ITS DISCONTENTS

Every cartoon ever published in *The New Yorker* is indexed and cross-referenced in the magazine's library. Until recently these files were updated by hand. Today this quaintly Dickensian practice has been replaced by computer imaging and floppy disks. The entire inventory is broken down into less than twenty categories, the largest being "Men" and "Women" (not surprisingly, since most cartoonists are either men or women) and in second place, "The Office."

Given the fact that most comic artists have never experienced salaried employment, the number of drawings that relate to the office place requires

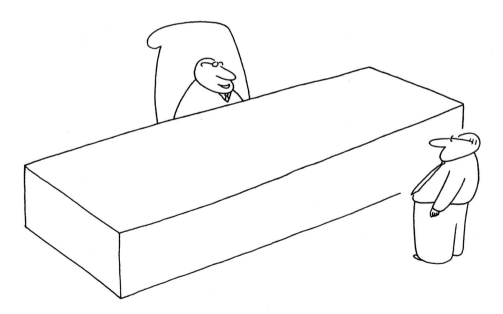

"Have you ever thought, Richards, how unfair it all is?"

explanation. Having done more than my share of such gags, I feel qualified to offer my own theory, and that is: power. Without putting the whole business of cartooning on the couch, it can be fairly said that cartoonists are, by and large, introspective, reclusive types. They prefer sniping at life's great targets behind the camouflage of humor to outright confrontation. (Barsotti makes explicit reference to this in his hand puppet series.) In my view, the Man Behind the Desk stands for all those vain, stone-hearted, all-powerful S.O.B.s that life inflicts on us. Since there are not enough bullets to shoot them all, the cartoonist performs a public service by cutting them down to size, one drawing at a time.

"Nothing for me, thanks. I'm a hand puppet."

"Oh, ha-ha-ha-ha-ha-ha, sir."

"They're too cute to fire. I just step on the ones that don't work out."

*"Someday, Jennings, you're going to
thank me for this."*

"And this will be your new home."

"Of course. Your reputation precedes you, sir."

"Wornal, take this plant out and kill it."

"Good news. You've been identified by your dental records."

UNEASY SITS THE CROWN

Charley in a curious
anticipation of
regal splendor.

Barsotti's King drawings raise the study of power figures to a whole new level of complexity. His royal "we" is a far more conflicted and interesting character than the standard office bully. He is devious and sentimental, ruthless yet subject to deep self-doubt, serene in his sovereignty but not above sharing a pizza with the palace guard.

With the notable exception of Bill Mauldin, Barsotti is the only cartoonist who ever attempted to seek power for himself. At the height of the Vietnam conflict, his antiwar sentiments led him to run unsuccessfully for Congress. Perhaps art and nature are not meant to mix. Surely, Charley has been a more effective spokesman for his views in the pages of *The New Yorker* then he could ever have been in the aisles of Congress.

"Albert the Great—what a joke."

"Anchovy."   "Make that half pepperoni and half anchovy."

"Oh, _no_, sir. I'm not just saying it because you're king. I think it's really very, very good."

"Why, this is fit for me!"

"It is we."

*"No, I wasn't abused,
but I cut off my father's head anyway."*

FROM ANTHROPOMORPHISM . . .

Every cartoonist has done at least a few talking animal gags, and ringing new changes on old standbys such as Humpty Dumpty or the dish running off with the spoon are often enough to get the juices flowing when inspiration flags. In the world of comic art, it is widely acknowledged that the all-time champion of anthropomorphic gags is Charles Barsotti. Talking plants and animals are cartoon staples, but Barsotti has single-handedly enlarged the anthropomorphic to include hot dogs, peanuts, bowling balls, claw hammers, and pasta. Working in this genre with no ground rules, Barsotti reveals a taste for wordplay, puns, and free association worthy of the Marx Brothers, an improbable mix of Ernie Kovacs and S.J. Perelman.

Giving tongue to the mute objects of the world seems to inspire Barsotti to greater and greater feats of imagination. Receiving a surprise phone call from Fusilli is sheer inspiration, but then how do we describe the series of drawings he did of businessmen rendered as empty cardboard boxes? There is a touch of divine madness here that connects these works to the cut-and-paste surrealism that he created in the eighties—to the great amusement of *The New Yorker*'s then editor Robert Gottlieb.

"Fusilli, you crazy bastard!
How are you?"

"Brazil nuts are my specialty."

"Gee, it was just meant to be a little constructive criticism."

"Fruit salad? Count me in!"

*"Good news, Bradshaw, I'm moving you to a branch office where we can
get the most out of your innate initiative and creativity."*

"Ooh, you have a tornado right <u>there</u>."

"Sorry, Pembroke, but Telford here is lavishly illustrated."

"Nuts to you, too."

"We won't really know anything until we find the black box."

"I thought it came with an acorn."

"Mr. Hoffman? Ed Hoffman? Your office has been trying to reach you, sir."

"Oh, that's a break.
His job description is right on top."

If Barsotti explores power through his kings and plutocrats, he reveals a gentler and more sentimental view of life through the adventures of his familiar pooch. Charley has revealed that his flop-eared mutt was inspired by a much-loved pet, Jiggs. Like his cartoon counterpart, Jiggs was earnest and well-intentioned, a Boy Scout in a dog suit.

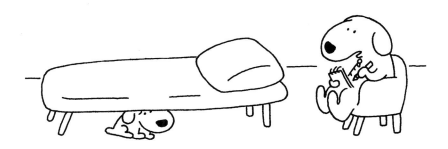

"And what do you think will happen if you __do__ get on the couch?"

"I understand you've learned some new tricks since you were here last."

"Not guilty. If they hadn't read Safire yet, Safire shouldn't have been on the floor."

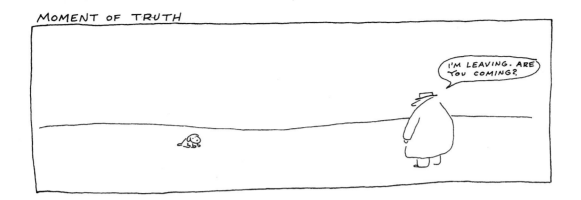

MOMENT OF TRUTH

I'M LEAVING. ARE YOU COMING?

"O.K., I'm on my way home."

"The bidding will start at eleven million dollars."

"Well, please look again, Operator. It's Fluffy—F-L-U-F-F-Y—and she lives in Larchmont."

"Not guilty, because puppies do these things."

LORENZ: You're a quick study. I remember how you picked up on Bob Gottlieb's interest in the marginally absurd. I noticed that you did some of those sort of collage things for *Punch* also.

BARSOTTI: Right, yes.

LORENZ: That was earlier, before the Gottlieb stuff.

BARSOTTI: It must have been. I don't recall for sure.
In fact, I joked that, in a way, *Punch* was sort of
a preparation for Gottlieb, only I didn't know it. When we got the news about Shawn leaving, besides being very upset I, along with everyone else, was wondering who the hell this Gottlieb guy was. I have to admit that I found out he had published an Englishman . . .

LORENZ: Glen Baxter.

BARSOTTI: Baxter's stuff, yeah. And so that was,
I guess, a clue.

LORENZ: That was a very good clue. Did you ever use that collage approach in the strips you did?

BARSOTTI: I did try some stuff in "Sally."
Yeah, a little bit, old engravings and so forth,
but not extensively. I mean, everything
seemed to be so damned conservative, we probably should have been bolder.

"You're home, dear—that's the main thing."

"Tell me again, J.B.,
what's the name of the new public relations firm you just hired?"

CHARLEY BARSOTTI IN
THE TWENTY-FIRST CENTURY

After twenty-six years under founder Harold Ross and thirty-six years under his successor, William Shawn, *The New Yorker* has now had three editors in the past ten years.

The effects of these continuing changes on the magazine's fortunes have been widely scrutinized in the press, but their impact on the magazine's contributors is seldom deemed newsworthy. From the perspective of *The New Yorker*'s cartoonists, it has been a wild ride. Robert Gottlieb, who replaced Shawn as editor in 1981, encouraged a mad-cap, off-the-wall humor that was a challenge to many of the established cartoonists. At the same time, he reintroduced cartoons on the magazine's covers, a practice Shawn had phased out. Under Tina Brown, *The New Yorker* expanded its use of other kinds of art. Full-page photographs and splashy color illustrations sometimes seemed to overwhelm the more modest black-and-white efforts of the cartoonists. How the magazine's art will evolve under its new editor, David Remnick, is once more a source of anxiety among the cartoonists. As in the past, most will survive, a few will flourish, and a few will be left behind. The winners will combine talent with tough-mindedness and the ability to adapt to changing circumstances.

Over his long career, Charley has demonstrated that he has these qualities in abundance. When Eustace Tilley rises to toast *The New Yorker*'s entrance to the millennium, it's a safe bet that Charles Barsotti will be seated nearby at the head table, sipping his San Pellegrino and pretending he likes it.

THE OLD BUCKAROO

IN 1978, Charley married his second wife, Ramoth. They make a remarkable twosome (their friends sometimes refer to them as "Barsotti Incorporated"). While Charley struggles with the demons of creativity in his studio, Rae tends to the nuts and bolts of an artist's life. She acts as book-keeper, librarian, research assistant, and agent ("Charley hates to haggle over money"). Rae also serves as Charley's number one

GRACEFULLY EXITING A BAR IN ODESSA

DIDN'T SPILL A DROP.

WHOMP!

fan. She often introduces herself as "the wife of the semi-famous *New Yorker* cartoonist Charles Barsotti." (That's the Southern "sem-eye" as in "semi-tough," with its full load of irony, as opposed to the neutral Northern "semmee" as in "semi-conscious.")

Rae also serves as social secretary, and nowhere are her skills more apparent than at the Barsotti's legendary Friday night gatherings in Kansas City. With Charley being part Italian and all Texan, his interest in food is only to be expected. Barbecue is his specialty. (He has long since conceded the palm for Italian cuisine to his sister Ann.) At their Friday night bashes, Charley works the smoker while Ramoth works the crowd: "I have a lot of ritual when

I barbecue. I put out the Texas flag and I douse the flames with a water pistol, just like Roy Rogers. I have three sauces for my ribs—one to marinate them in, one to work with while they're cooking, and another one that I put on the table. I suppose that's redundant, but I like it." So do his guests, who claim (*pace* Calvin Trillin) that Charley serves the best barbecue in Kansas City. A modest man, Charley defers to the grill meisters of the Lone Star State: "For real barbecue, take I-35 south till you hit Lockhart, Texas."

LORENZ: Those Friday night bashes that you and Rae used to throw became legendary in Kansas City.

BARSOTTI: Well, semi-legendary.

LORENZ: Tell me about them. You were the cook?

BARSOTTI: Maybe occasionally, but mostly Ramoth did the cooking—things like mussels or chili. When it was barbecue, I cooked.

LORENZ: What kind of music did you feature at these parties? Country and western, I guess.

BARSOTTI: Whatever Ramoth would put on. Yes, it would have been a lot of country and

THE FRIENDLY WEST

HOT ENOUGH FOR YOU, BILL?

HOTTER'N AUNT NELL AT A TENT MEETING.

SOUTHERN BAPTIST–NORTHERN ITALIAN PASTA

Sauté two pounds of ground beef.

In blender, chop:
  3 or 4 carrots
  1 bell green pepper
  1 medium onion
  3 stalks celery (with the leaves)

Add to browned ground beef the above, plus:
  1 small can tomato sauce
  8 ounces water
  1 can tomatoes, including juice
  1 bay leaf
  1 tablespoon paprika
  Salt and pepper to taste (Start with two
    tablespoons of salt. You may want to
    add more.)
  1/2 teaspoon oregano
  1/8 teaspoon thyme
  Some fresh parsley, chopped

Simmer for one and one-half hours.

Sauté some fresh mushrooms and add for the last 20 minutes.

That's the sauce. Now cook up some pasta and off you go.

ANN ARMENTROUT'S* CHILI

  2 tablespoons oil (olive oil, bacon
    drippings, lard or butter)
  1 large onion, sautéed until soft
  3 pounds of lean beef or venison
    (or half beef, half venison perhaps),
    cut into thumb-size pieces or coarsely
    ground

Mix with:
  3 garlic cloves, chopped
  5 tablespoons chili powder
  1 tablespoon ground comino

Mix with the sautéed onion and brown.

Add:
  2 teaspoons of salt
  1 tablespoon paprika
  3 cups water

Cook for two hours.

* That's my sister. She's the last word in Texas chili around here. Ramoth is a wonderful cook and she makes some stuff that we call chili. It's very good, but it's very different.

"I wonder, sir, if you would indulge me in a rather unusual request?"

western. Willie Nelson, that sort of thing.

LORENZ: Did you ever have live music?

BARSOTTI: Well, we didn't try to stop anyone.

LORENZ: And I understand there were sing-alongs.

BARSOTTI: Well, that probably is true.

LEISURE TIME

I THINK THIS SHOULD PROVE TO EVERYONE'S SATISFACTION THAT I POSSESS CERTAIN QUALITIES OF PLAYFULNESS.

LORENZ: In other words, anything could have happened if the evening was long enough.

BARSOTTI: That's true also. One Friday we were working with some Japanese advertising executives. We were having trouble communicating, even though we had an interpreter. Around five o'clock I said to Ramoth, I think what we really need is steaks and Scotch. Those were the old days, before we started counting calories. So we had some steaks, and we had a lot of Scotch. It was a huge success.

LORENZ: You found a common language, right?

BARSOTTI: Well, Ramoth did. By the end of the evening, she was teaching them the Texas two-step.

LORENZ: I understand there were also impromptu readings of poetry. Someone mentioned you reciting some T.S. Eliot, "The Love Song of J. Alfred Prufrock."

BARSOTTI: Hmm? Maybe.

LORENZ: I mean, it's nothing to be ashamed of, God knows. Do you have a deep interest in poetry?

BARSOTTI: No, not deep. A shallow interest, maybe. Actually, I was also the titular poetry editor of the *Post*. I say "titular" because it folded before I was given any poetry to edit. These readings came about one Fourth of July as something Rae set up. She said everyone had to be ready to make a suitable speech or gesture of some kind. I thought it was going to be a grand bust, but it worked. And ironically, one of the best was from our English friend Michael Wolff.

LORENZ: On the one hand you have deep roots in Texas and country, and on the other hand you're a very sophisticated person. Your friend Emerson once called you a "supersophisticated yokel."

"Go ahead, finish your beer."

BARSOTTI: You know, somebody else pointed that out. When I came out with the Texas book in 1986, he said, "You finally found a way to get your pickup into Harvard Square."

SAD MUSIC

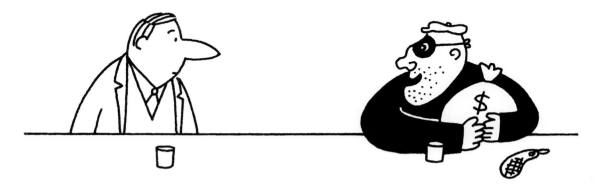

"In a sense, yes, I'm guilty."

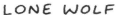

LONE WOLF

LONESOME COWBOY

TEXAS
NO MORE LOLLYGAGGING AROUND! TODAY'S THE DAY!
HOUSTON CITY LIMITS
YES, THIS IS THE DAY OUR HERO, MAYNARD, THE YOUNG URBAN EXECUTIVE TRAINEE, BEGINS HIS QUEST!
YESSIR, TODAY I FIND MY TRUE LOVE...
WELCOME TO AUSTIN
TODAY SOMEWHERE, SOMEHOW, WHOEVER SHE IS, I'M GONNA FIND MY LOVE...
...THE TEXAS CHAINSAW CHEERLEADER!
WACO 5 MILES
BOYOHBOY! WE'RE GONNA BE SO HAPPY! WE'RE GONNA BE SO SILLY! WE'RE GONNA LAUGH AND GIGGLE ALL THE TIME! I CAN'T WAIT 'TIL I FIND HER!
DALLAS CITY LIMITS
OH, THE POOR THING!
IT'S TOO LATE.
SHE'S BEEN CAPTURED BY YANKEES!
WELCOME TO CHICAGO
MORAL:
LIKE ASPHALT, YOU CAN COVER A LOT OF GROUND AND STILL BE AS DUMB AS WHEN YOU STARTED.

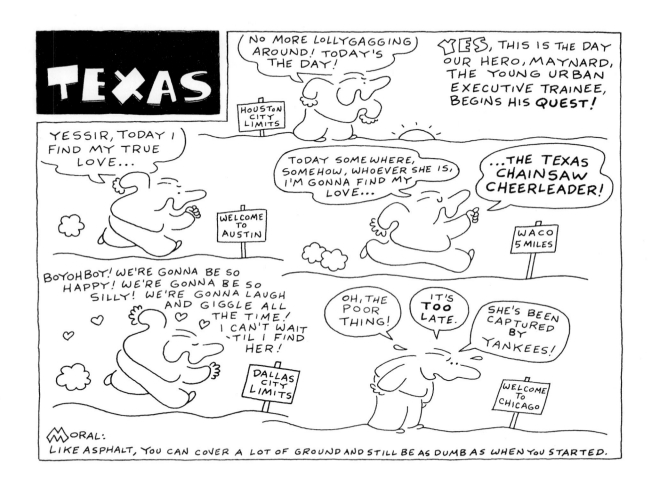

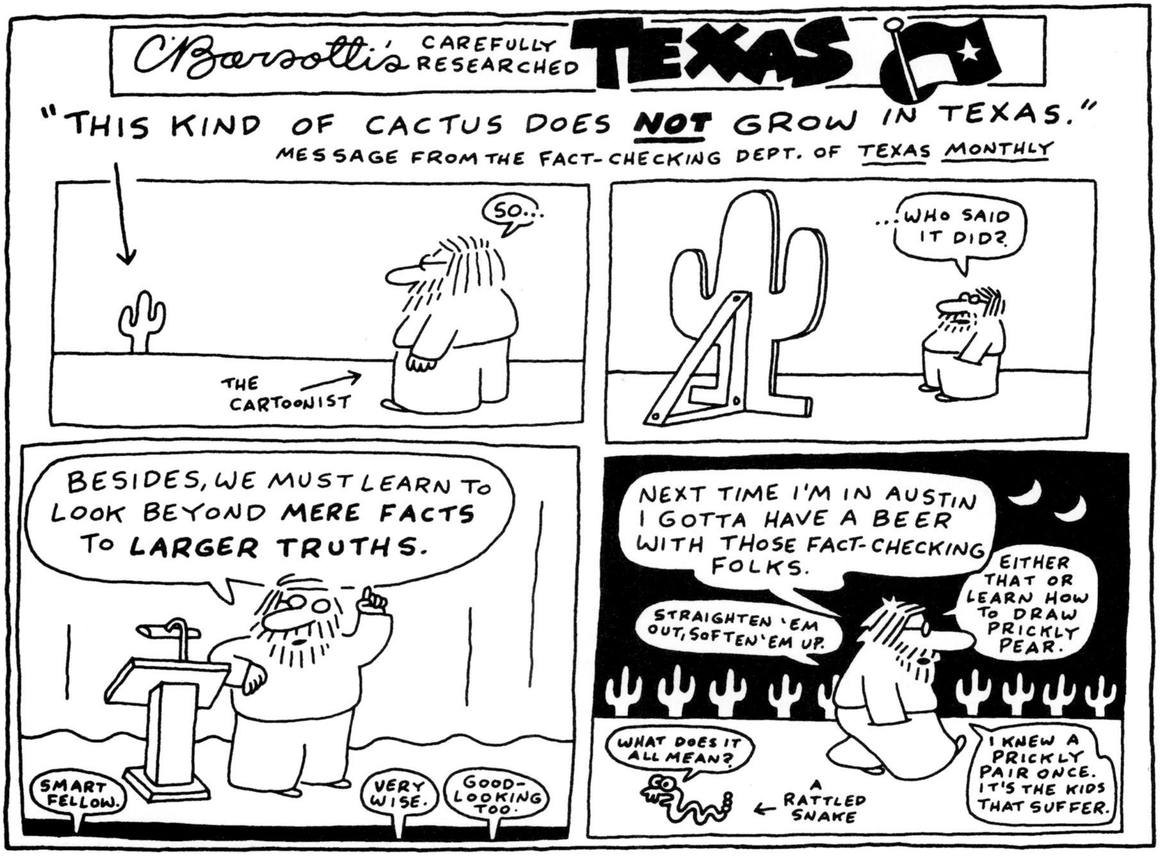
C. Barsotti's CAREFULLY RESEARCHED TEXAS
"THIS KIND OF CACTUS DOES NOT GROW IN TEXAS."
MESSAGE FROM THE FACT-CHECKING DEPT. OF TEXAS MONTHLY
SO...
THE CARTOONIST
...WHO SAID IT DID?
BESIDES, WE MUST LEARN TO LOOK BEYOND MERE FACTS TO LARGER TRUTHS.
SMART FELLOW.
VERY WISE.
GOOD-LOOKING TOO.
NEXT TIME I'M IN AUSTIN I GOTTA HAVE A BEER WITH THOSE FACT-CHECKING FOLKS.
STRAIGHTEN 'EM OUT, SOFTEN 'EM UP.
EITHER THAT OR LEARN HOW TO DRAW PRICKLY PEAR.
WHAT DOES IT ALL MEAN?
A RATTLED SNAKE
I KNEW A PRICKLY PAIR ONCE. IT'S THE KIDS THAT SUFFER.

TAKING A STAND

W hen cartoonists gather together, the favored topic is not sports or the parlous state of the business—it's politics. The conversation often gets heated, but if everyone talks about politics I only know one cartoonist who ever attempted to do anything about it—Charles Barsotti.

LORENZ: Tell me a bit more about that side of your life. You once ran for the U.S. Congress?

BARSOTTI: Yeah, I felt very strongly about the Vietnam War. I ran for the Democratic nomination as an antiwar statement, and much to my amazement I got it. That was in Kansas in '72. Kansas was not a hotbed of antiwar activity, and I got murdered in the

Despite being rebuffed at the polls, Charley has never wavered in his commitment to "truth, justice, and the American way."

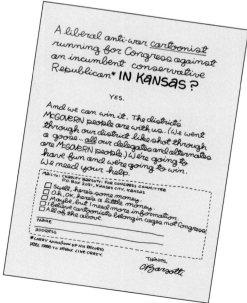

A liberal anti-war cartoonist running for Congress against an incumbent conservative Republican* IN KANSAS?

YES.

And we can win it. The district's McGOVERN people are with us. (We went through our district like shot through a goose... all our delegates and alternates are McGOVERN people.) We're going to have fun and we're going to win. We need your help.

Mail to: CHARLEY BARSOTTI FOR CONGRESS COMMITTEE
P.O. Box 2031, KANSAS CITY, KANSAS

☐ Swell, here's some money.
☐ Oh, OK, here's a little money.
☐ Maybe, but I need more information.
☐ I believe cartoonists belong in cages not Congress!
☐ All of the above.

NAME

ADDRESS

*LARRY WINN (look up his record)
FEEL FREE TO XEROX LIKE CRAZY.

THANKS,
Barsotti

101

general election. I am absolutely not cut out for politics. In the end, I just stood for Congress and some people got a chance to cast an antiwar vote. That's about all. It was a silly thing to do, but it was well intentioned. I had no ambition to be in Congress except for the stupid war. If anything about it surprised me, it might have been the shock of being taken as an idealistic young fellow one day to being a highly suspect pol the next.

I have a friend who ran successfully for county attorney three times here in Kansas City. He's good at campaigning and I begrudgingly admire that, but it's not for me.

"I'm voting my pocketbook again this year. How about you, Winstead?"

NOT BY GAGS ALONE

LORENZ: As far as I know, you're also the only cartoonist who ever had a restaurant named after him.

BARSOTTI: That's neat. What is that wonderful word in the dictionary? We never use it in conversation, but it's when you have something named after you. Epony—

LORENZ: Eponymous.

BARSOTTI: Yeah. Bill and Ellen Crook from Texas—great friends, Bill died recently—invested in a local restaurant a few years back, and at some point decided that they wanted to add a second one, with Italian food. Bill called to ask permission to name it Barsotti's. I was delighted. My signature was up over the entrance in neon lights. I understand that when it closed, some college kid tossed a beer bottle through the lights. *Sic transit* and all that.

LORENZ: And it was decorated with blowups of your drawings, right?

BARSOTTI: Right, and I decorated the menu. So anyway, for a while there was an Italian restaurant in San Marcos called Barsotti's, and you could get very good food there.

Comments on a "Barsotti's" menu suggest that the art-work was as palatable as the food.

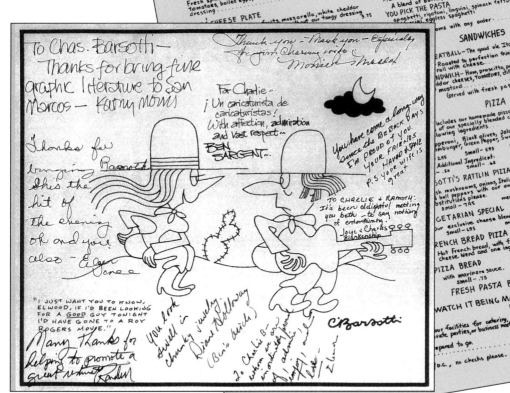

"You've been selected to appear in the forthcoming edition of 'Who's Who on the Lone Prairie.'"

FRONTIERSMAN

"I'd like to report some bad guys."

ART IS LONG
(BUT THE FED EX MAN
IS WAITING)

Charley Barsotti wrestles with his Muse in a large, but not large enough studio surrounded by the basic tools of his craft: a drawing table, a fax machine, a computer, and a taboret to hold his pens, pencils, and cigars. Books and magazines fill the shelves that line the walls and spill over onto the floor. A bulletin board charts various works in progress and displays memorable items clipped from the press, including: "WORK FROM HOME IN YOUR UNDERWEAR!" (Actually, Charley more often works in his pajamas.)

GENIUS AT MIDNIGHT

I'M GOING TO GET A NEW AGENT.

There are plenty of windows, but the shades are usually drawn. The walls are decorated with prints by Miró and Matisse, and posters for films by Chaplin (*The Great Dictator*) and Harold Lloyd. A large model of the infamous Bee Gee racing plane hangs from the ceiling, and the remaining wall space is decorated with gargoyles, clocks, wind-up toys, and a piece of Russian constructivist sculpture. A standout in this wildly mixed antipasto is an Italian poster that improbably blends Mickey Mouse and Miró. But if the decorating style is early W.C. Fields, the functionality is as up to date as the latest modem. Despite the apparent chaos, Charley is famously prolific and punctual.

Artwork is dispatched by courier here and abroad, and the telephone, computer, and fax machine often compete for the artist's attention.

"So you've read my books and you've brought wine. Good."

BARSOTTI: There's a lot to be said for the Luddites. "Good morning. Are there any faxes?" is a pretty standard a.m. greeting in our house. The phone, the fax, and Fed Ex, as Rae asks, "What did we do without them?" In the early days of developing the Niceday image and packaging, the work was heavy and intense. Mark-Steen was in London and I was in Kansas City, and we developed a lasting friendship pushing stuff back and forth across the Atlantic by fax. He was marvelous at his end. I once went into the studio to find that he'd faxed me my breakfast. You've got to love a guy who'll fax you breakfast.

"Old?" She laughed. "I don't think of you as old."

"With all due respect, Reverend Falwell, I will continue to make out the list of who's been naughty and nice just as I have always done."

"We're the Duderstadt brothers. I believe we have a table for four."

COURTING THE MUSE

A cartoonist's greatest reward is neither fame nor fortune, both of which may be more successfully pursued elsewhere. It is the creation of a drawing that prompts other cartoonists to say, "Why didn't I think of that?" These ideas seem to spring full-blown from the artist's unconscious, and often the artist's own reaction is, "Hasn't this been thought of by someone else?" Almost every cartoonist has experienced these transcendent moments. Barsotti seems to have had more than his share, but it is what the artist can produce while the muse is off having a beer that distinguished the best cartoonists from the run of the mill.

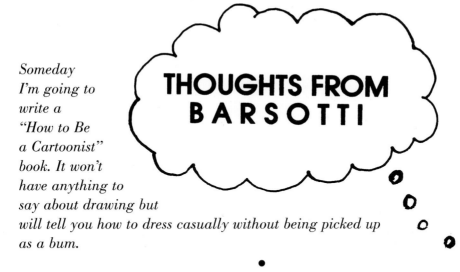

THOUGHTS FROM BARSOTTI

Someday I'm going to write a "How to Be a Cartoonist" book. It won't have anything to say about drawing but will tell you how to dress casually without being picked up as a bum.

•

I will reveal the true history of cartooning from the earliest times when cartoonists drew on air. This was known as the Golden Age because no one could prove the drawings weren't as funny as the artists claimed they were.

•

Eventually, of course, editors came along and messed things up by passing gas through the air cartoons. Since then, things haven't changed that much.

•

I will also include a few of the hard truths I've learned about the business over the years. For example: Talent is okay, but denial is critical.

•

It's been written that creative work is the hardest work of all. It goes without saying that this was written by artists, not ditchdiggers.

"My first husband wrote five thousand words a day,
every day, rain or shine."

The cartoonist's weekly batch, the raw material of his career, which consists of anything from eight to twenty sketches, is the result of long, lonely hours spent flipping through magazines, reading the newspapers, staring out the window, sharpening pencils, and drinking coffee. How all this translates into funny ideas on paper is a mystery, of course, and the rituals surrounding the process are as varied and individual as the cartoonists themselves. Barsotti's method is to take a piece of paper and a pencil, stare at one and fondle the other, and eventually begin doodling until an idea begins to form. He pursues the idea until he feels it has completely resolved itself, and then sketches it up. He then takes another piece of paper and starts the same process once more.

"Trouble, J.B. Everyone in Accounting is molting."

LORENZ: What are your work habits? Do you have a regular schedule?

BARSOTTI: Well, an accountant would laugh at the idea of regularity in my schedule.

LORENZ: Do you try to work a certain amount of time every day, or are you one of those people who have to depend on a deadline to get anything done?

BARSOTTI: Somewhere in between. There always seem to be plenty of deadlines, and that's all to the good, but I don't have to depend on them. I try to keep things in order and priorities straight.

I draw with a Rapidograph pen on two-ply, regular-finish Strathmore paper. I know you've described my sketches as "tiny," but they're actually 7 ½" x 9 ½".

LORENZ: Size matters.

"I'm sorry, Wilson, but I liked you better before your therapy."

BARSOTTI: I'd better let that pass.

LORENZ: When do you do your *New Yorker* work?

BARSOTTI: I usually start working on *The New Yorker* on Friday. Most of the time, I start with something that's bugging me and just doodle around until an idea gels. Then I draw it up, take another piece of paper, and start the next one.

LORENZ: In addition to your published work, I understand that you're now peddling your stuff on the electronic highway.

BARSOTTI: Oh, that's really my daughter Jean's project. I know diddly about this computer business, but she's a whiz. We offer T-shirts, coffee mugs— that kind of stuff—on-line. I do know that we get fantastic e-mail, but if you want to know how it works you can ask her. The website is www.barsotti.com.

CAGED FURY

"*I'm not angry, I'm just very disappointed.*"

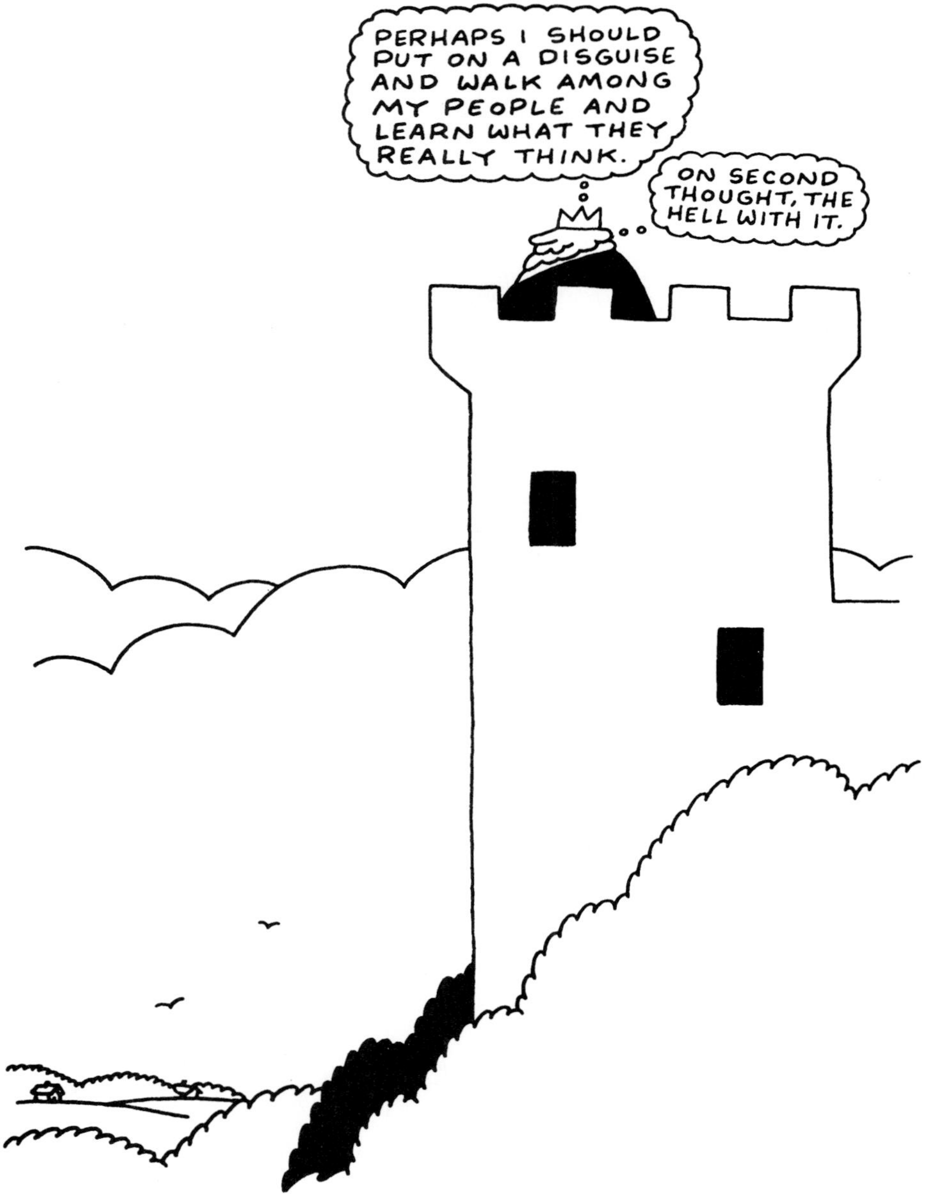
PERHAPS I SHOULD PUT ON A DISGUISE AND WALK AMONG MY PEOPLE AND LEARN WHAT THEY REALLY THINK.
ON SECOND THOUGHT, THE HELL WITH IT.

STYLE MAKES THE MAN

Cartoonists spend a great deal of time analyzing their own work. This is less a question of vanity than a part of the creative process itself. But if artists are the shrewdest critics of their own work, they are also generally reluctant to share these insights with the public at large. (A notable exception is Picasso, who remains the most reliable critic of his own work.) This places the artist in an awkward position. On the one hand, he or she would like the public to acknowledge that what they do involves a great deal of hard work. On the other hand, there is something satisfying about being perceived as in the possession of a rare and special gift.

"Very good, Benson. That's what I want to see."

In addition to the "funny papers," Charley's gift was nourished by the classic radio comedians of the 1930s and '40s. Every Sunday evening the Barsotti family gathered around the Philco to enjoy the antics of Jack Benny, Fred Allen, and Edgar Bergen and Charlie McCarthy (Charley changed the spelling of his first name to distance himself from the celebrated ventriloquist's alter ego).

Charley has favored a pared-down, minimalist style from the beginning of his career (he describes his artwork as "post-cluttered"). His pen line is uninflected, and he avoids the use of half-tone, conventional perspective, and anything else that might puncture the two-dimensional surface of his drawings. Richness and variety are added by the judicious use of blacks and the occasional comic strip–style box.

Like all the best cartoonists, Charley chooses his subjects to suit his style. In his comic world, the pace is never hectic. His people amble down the sidewalk and his punch lines are delivered in the measured cadences of a weather report. He avoids all high-energy types. No small children, high-strung teenagers, or battling spouses. In fact, his work is notable for its absence of such familiar comic clichés as flying saucers and desert islands. The old favorites he does turn to appear without their familiar doppelgängers— heaven but not hell, romance but not sex, dogs but not cats.

With his modest road company and deliberate style, Charley continues to produce work of surprising range and variety. Less may not always be more, but, at least in Charley's case, it's more than enough.

WHY THEY HAVE SPRING TRAINING

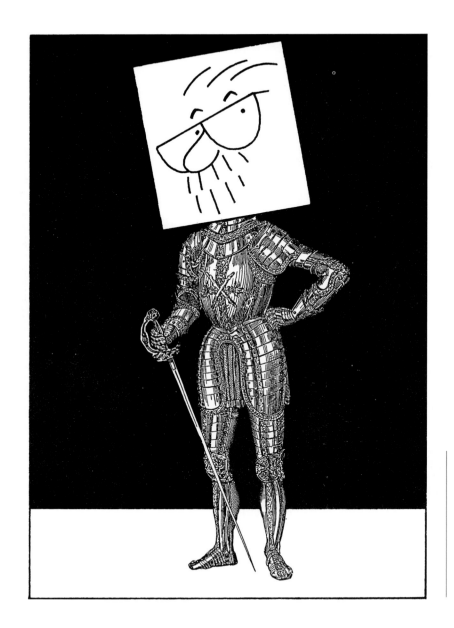

With the notable exception of the Dada-like collages he produced for Gottlieb's *New Yorker*, Barsotti rarely strays from his spare, linear style. The work on these pages demonstrates a more experimental approach, used occasionally in his op-ed page work but seldom in his more familiar gag cartoons.

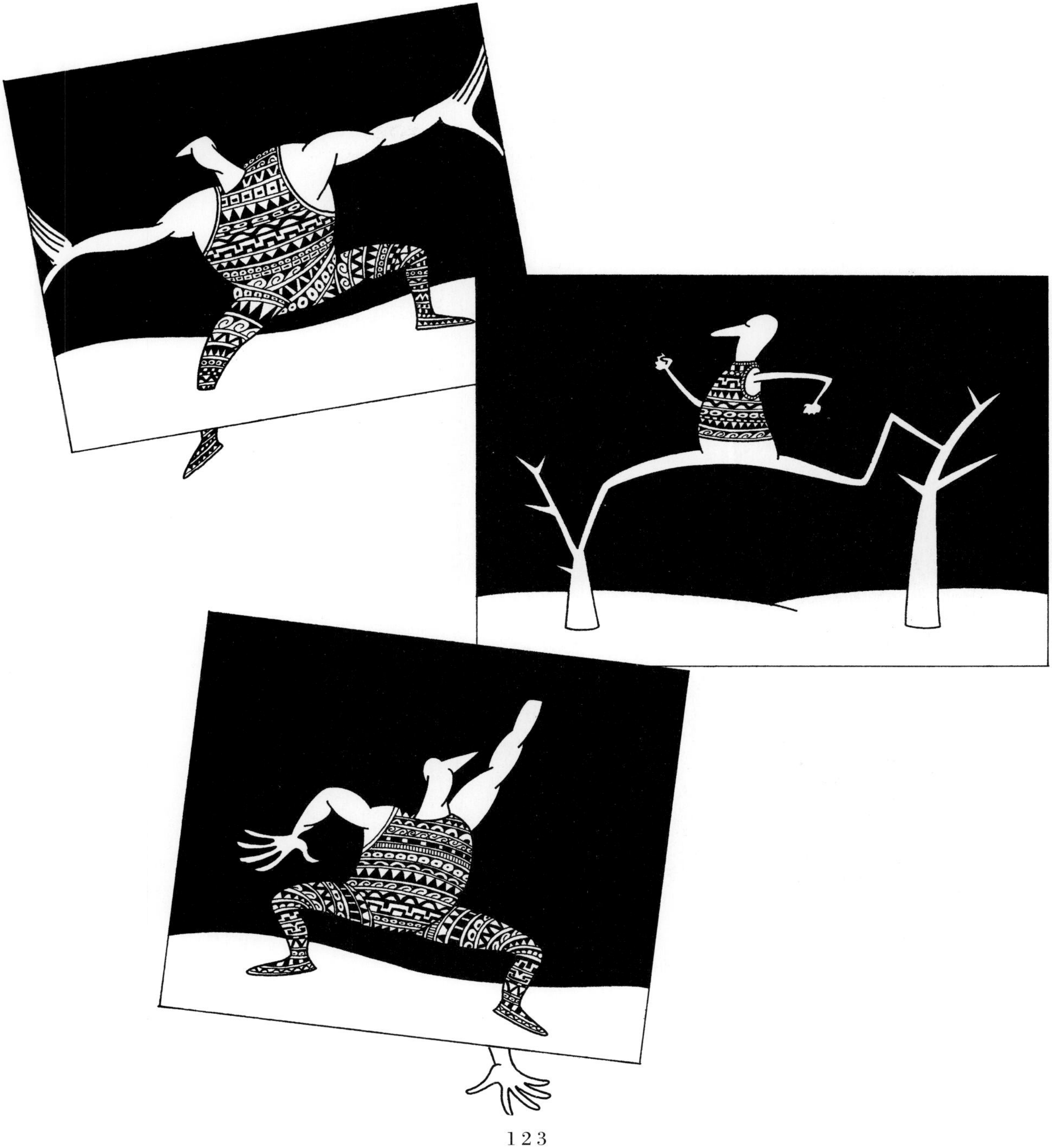

A PROPHET HONORED

If Charley's credentials as a "good old boy" are still suspect in some quarters, his bona fides have been enthusiastically accepted in his old hometown. His college has invited him back twice to receive awards.

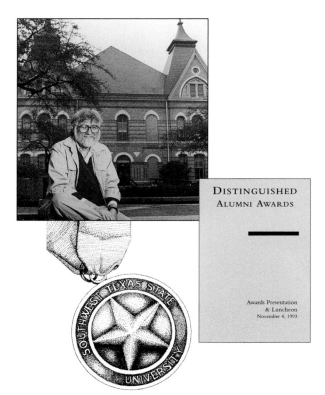

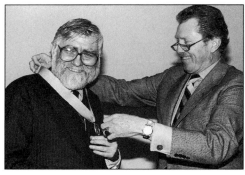

Barsotti with S.T.S. president Robert L. Hardesty (above) and his old college pal Bill Porterfield (below).

DISTINGUISHED
ALUMNI AWARDS

Awards Presentation
& Luncheon
November 4, 1993

President's Excellence Award

Mr. Charles Barsotti
Southwest Texas Alumni and
Nationally Syndicated Cartoonist

February 25, 1987

SUPPORTING THE HABIT

THE PECULIAR PLEASURE of magazine cartooning is a kind of indulgence that most artists need to subsidize by other kinds of work. During his career, Barsotti has written and illustrated books, created ad campaigns, and drawn comic strips while working for publications as diverse as *Punch, The New Yorker, Playboy, Barron's, USA Today,* the *Time* op-ed page, and *Texas Monthly.*

LORENZ: Tell me about your experiences with *USA Today*.

BARSOTTI: It started one hot, steamy summer day. This fellow whom I didn't know at the time, Ron Martin, called and said they were starting a newspaper and would I come to Washington, D.C., to discuss cartoons. I said it's too hot

in D.C. He said that he'd grown up in Missouri and I couldn't kid him that it was any cooler in Kansas City. My work was in the prototype and in nearly every issue until nine years later, when I got another surprise telephone call from the editor of *USA Today*. Another editor, to be sure, and one who didn't think cartoons were such a splendid idea. We're supposed to get used to stuff like that.

LORENZ: You covered the 1984 Republican convention for them in Dallas.

BARSOTTI: Yeah, the Republicans were renominating Reagan and couldn't have been happier, so there wasn't much to draw about. There was a moment that I treasure, though. I was walking down a hallway in the press section and the publisher of the paper came loping by. He shouted, "Hey, Charley, you're in the ear!" I thought, for Christ's sake, what did he say? *In my ear?* What brought that on? Who knew newspaper talk? He meant one of my drawings plugging the cartoons inside was going to be on the front page up beside the logo—a really nice place to be, as it turns out.

"My God, what time is it?"

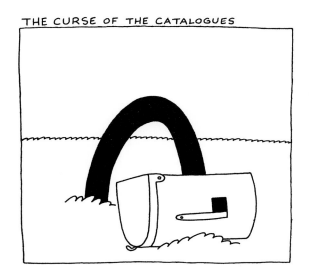

THE CURSE OF THE CATALOGUES

"It's just as well, Hopkins, I was going to fire you anyway."

THE ENGLISH CONNECTION

Occasionally, the cartoonist's hard-found work is augmented by the serendipitous. For Barsotti, an unexpected phone call from London one afternoon led to a challenging new field of activity that continues to expand.

LORENZ: Your work abroad began with Michael Wolff. When did he first get in touch with you?

BARSOTTI: Maybe ten years ago. He told me later that he was very nervous about calling and had been putting it off. He called about three or four o'clock my time, and of course I was working. Back then I wasn't sure what the time difference was, but listening to this guy talk I was convinced that the pubs had just closed. It turns out that he always talks that way. I didn't know what to make of it, so I said, well, send me some samples of what you do. He sent me some stuff, and I was very impressed.

LORENZ: This was his own design firm?

BARSOTTI: Right. Wolff's a leading designer in the U.K., and at this point he was on his own. Among the things he sent was a calendar for a consortium of banks called 3i. It's not a typical bank calendar; it's a big deal. They thought their cartoons weren't funny enough. I did all fifty-two drawings the first year. Rae and I went over to England for the launch. They had a show of my stuff at one of the clubs—I think it's called the Art Club— and one thing led to another. W.H. Smith bought five office-supply firms and wanted to combine them under the name Niceday. Wolff thought to

January 1994

M T W T F S S M T W T F S S
1 2 3 4 5 6 7 8 9
10 11 12 13 14 15 16 17 18 19 20 21 22 23
24 25 26 27 28 29 30 31

Chinese New Year and Year of the Dog - January 24th
Niceday ruler

August 1994

M T W T F S S M T W T F S S
1 2 3 4 5 6 7 8 9 10 11 12 13 **14**
15 16 17 18 19 20 21 22 23 24 25 26 27 28
29 30 31

Edinburgh Festival · August 14th to September 3rd
Niceday highlighters

Left: Pages from the Niceday calendar—an unexpected echo of Hallmark.

129

use my cartoon pup as part of the packaging. I flew over and worked for a week at Newell & Sorrell, a design firm, with Wolff and a talented madman named Mark-Steen Adamson. Although I loved the idea, I didn't really think the business people would go along with it in the end. They did, and it's been a terrific project. We won a bunch of awards (which the design firm got, not me), and since then we've designed hundreds of packages (each bit of Niceday packaging has a cartoon done expressly for it) and done ads and promotions—the pup's on the sides of lorries and even on a hot-air balloon. Now Niceday had been bought by a French firm and it's Guilbert-Niceday and we're redesigning packages for Europe.

I've done quite a lot of work in the U.K.: billboards for *The Evening Standard*, ads including a TV commercial for British Telecom, and stuff for British Aerospace. I had a cartoon on the back cover of the program for the reopening of Shakespeare's Globe Theater. The Bard and me, how about that?

BARSOTTI: On one of my trips to London I met Sheena Boyd, who was then the cartoon editor of *Punch*. She liked my stuff and bought a ton of it, including some covers.

LORENZ: I see a sort of freedom in the drawings you've done for *Punch*, in both the ideas and the drawings, as if you really felt you could let yourself go.

BARSOTTI: Yes, I did. Maybe part of that was because their circulation was about six or seven, and it was

"Try a French zoo. French zoos will take anything that wanders in."

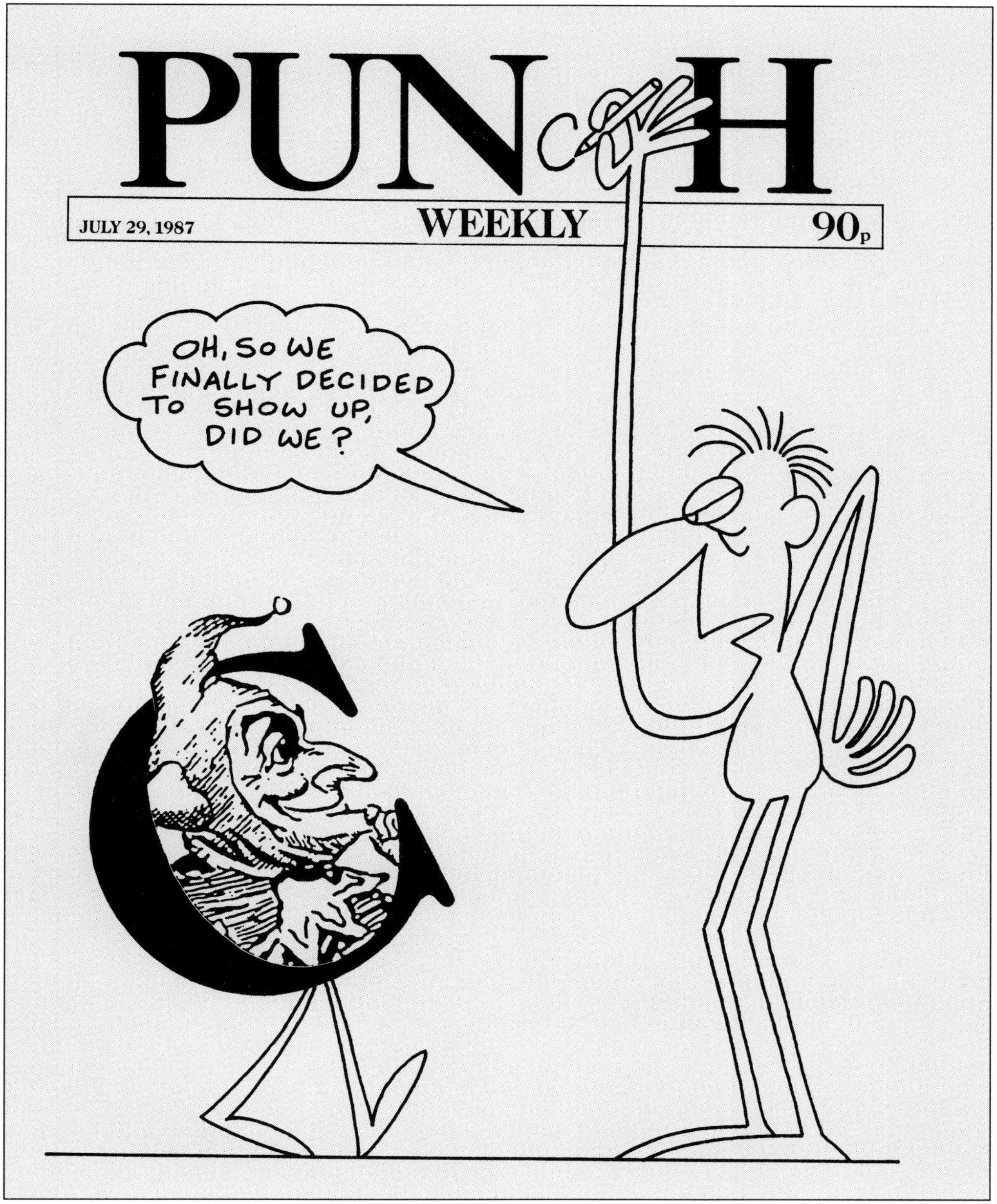
PUNCH
JULY 29, 1987
WEEKLY
90p
OH, SO WE FINALLY DECIDED TO SHOW UP, DID WE?

overseas, and I liked the cartoon editor. We got on wonderfully well. She was a lot of fun.

LORENZ: Well, they looked like they were fun. You also did covers for them?

BARSOTTI: I think I only did a couple of covers, and only one was intentionally a cover.

LORENZ: Mr. Punch?

BARSOTTI: Right, that was meant to be a cover. I've got that one framed. The other one she surprised me with—it was a blown-up cartoon.

When the Royal Mail (the British postal service) decided to issue a group of stamps with cartoons on them, the English cartoonist Mal did three, Charley Barsotti did three, and Jack Ziegler and Leo Cullum did one each.

"Oh, stop whimpering,
I could have fired you during hunting season."

"It's as uncanny as it's distressing, Humphreys, but day by day
you look more and more like your filofax."

"For God's sake, Elwood, the Queen's going to be here for tea in ten minutes and you're still in your robe and pyjamas."

"There, I did it. I called Buckingham Palace, but they said, no, you couldn't come play with the Corgis because you're just a mutt."

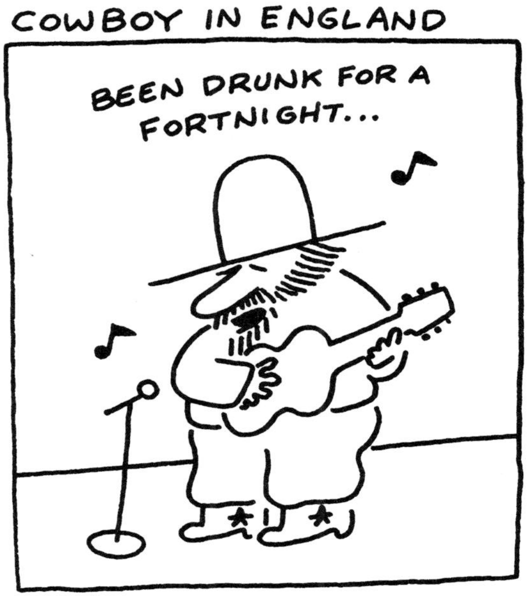
COWBOY IN ENGLAND
BEEN DRUNK FOR A FORTNIGHT...

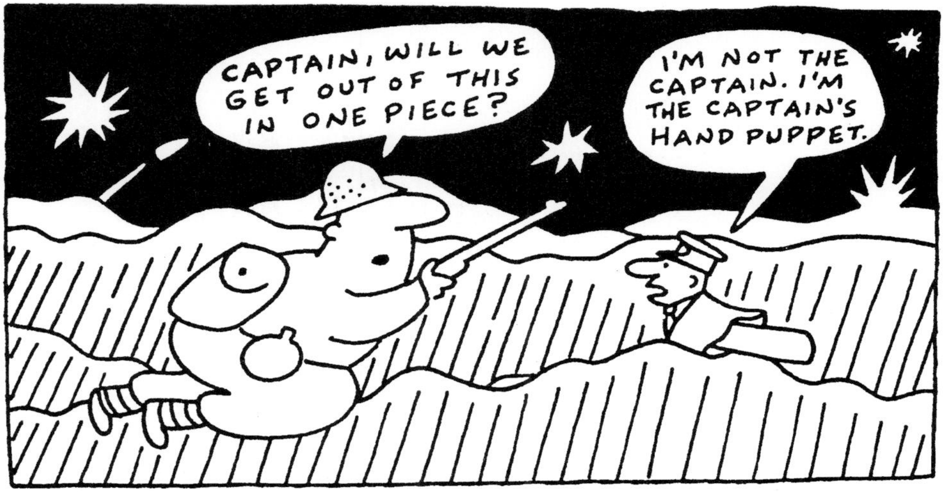
CAPTAIN, WILL WE GET OUT OF THIS IN ONE PIECE?
I'M NOT THE CAPTAIN. I'M THE CAPTAIN'S HAND PUPPET.

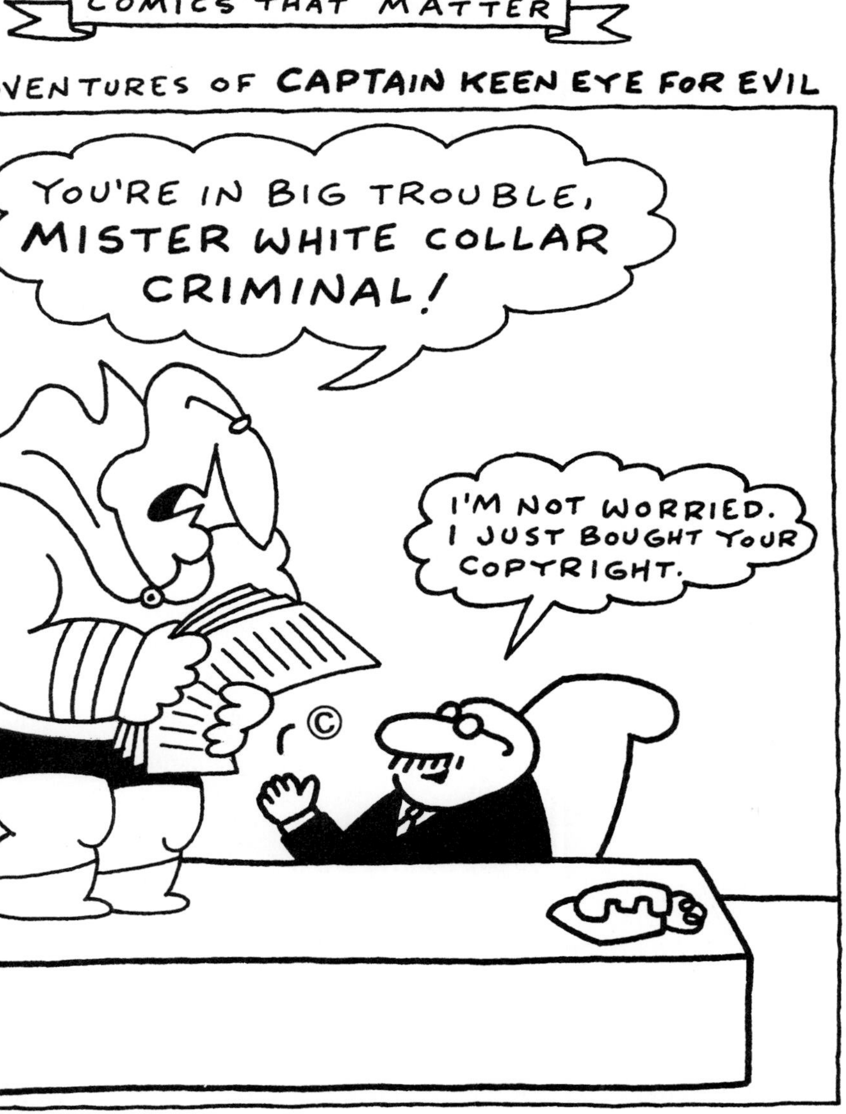
COMICS THAT MATTER
THE ADVENTURES OF CAPTAIN KEEN EYE FOR EVIL
I HAVE THE DOCUMENTS!
I HAVE THE PROOF!
YOU'RE IN BIG TROUBLE, MISTER WHITE COLLAR CRIMINAL!
I'M NOT WORRIED. I JUST BOUGHT YOUR COPYRIGHT.

"Never mind, I'll come back later."

REALITY CHECK

LORENZ: Has anyone ever approached you about using your work in other media? Making film, or adapting it for television?

BARSOTTI: No, not other than commercials or advertising. At one point there was some fella who thought he could make a theatrical production out of Emma June, but that didn't work out.

LORENZ: What about your dog?

BARSOTTI: The dog, of course, is being used in England extensively at Niceday, and Jean, my daughter, has produced some T-shirts. That's worked out fairly well.

LORENZ: What about you? Have you ever thought about trying to take some of the characters that you've developed over the years and using them in some other way, say, on television?

BARSOTTI: No, I haven't. Other than daydreaming.

LORENZ: Well, it all starts with daydreaming, right?

BARSOTTI: That's true, isn't it? I just realized as soon as I said it that that's where it starts. No, I don't think I have quite the right thing for it yet. You know, I keep in my studio a small headline from *The New York Times* several years ago—TV MOVIES OF AMY FISHER ARE HITS ON THREE NETWORKS— just to remind me what reality is.

"Have the fish. Fish is brain food."

"PERSONAL BEST"

Selections made by the artist's
favorite editor—himself.

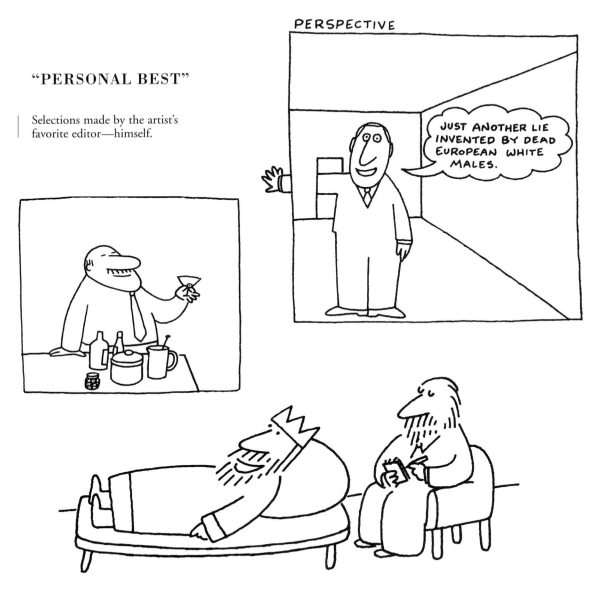

"It's a cage. It's gilded, and I love it."

"It's from MOMA.
You've been accepted for the permanent collection."

"I exiled the lot of them. How are your kids?"

"They moved my bowl."

"War, J.B., is the continuation of business by other means."

"Are you ready to play 'Give me a break, I was only human'?"

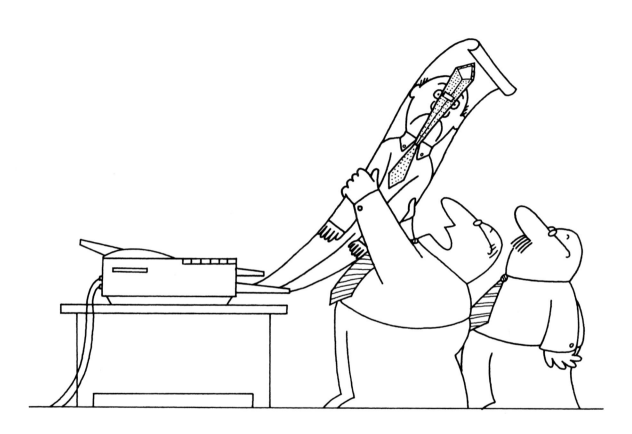

"*My God, there's been a terrible accident in our Chicago office!*"

"*Face it, Herb, you're one of those people who peaked in high school.*"

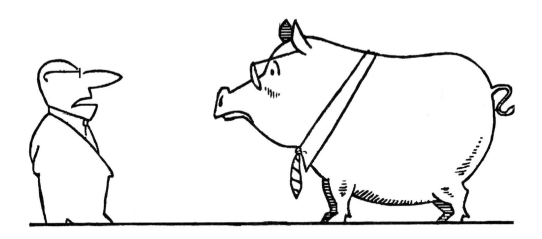

"Basic economics—sometimes the parts are worth more than the whole."

LAST WORD

Barsotti has been described as a social satirist, an inspired clown, and Kansas City's answer to James Thurber. William Emerson, editor of *The Saturday Evening Post*, once characterized Charley this way: "He's not sanforized or dry-cleaned. . . . I think he sort of speaks to the yearnings for a simpler, more basic view of things. There is a great suspicion that life has gotten out of hand. I think that Charley operates artistically at the center of that suspicion and he's able to create a lot of comic and ironic effect."

Charley's own view of his work is characteristically modest: "I suppose it's satire, but it's not very direct. When I fill out the Fed Ex form, one of the questions is 'Does this package contain dangerous materials?' I wish it did, but if I had to answer I'd say, 'No, just whimsy.'"

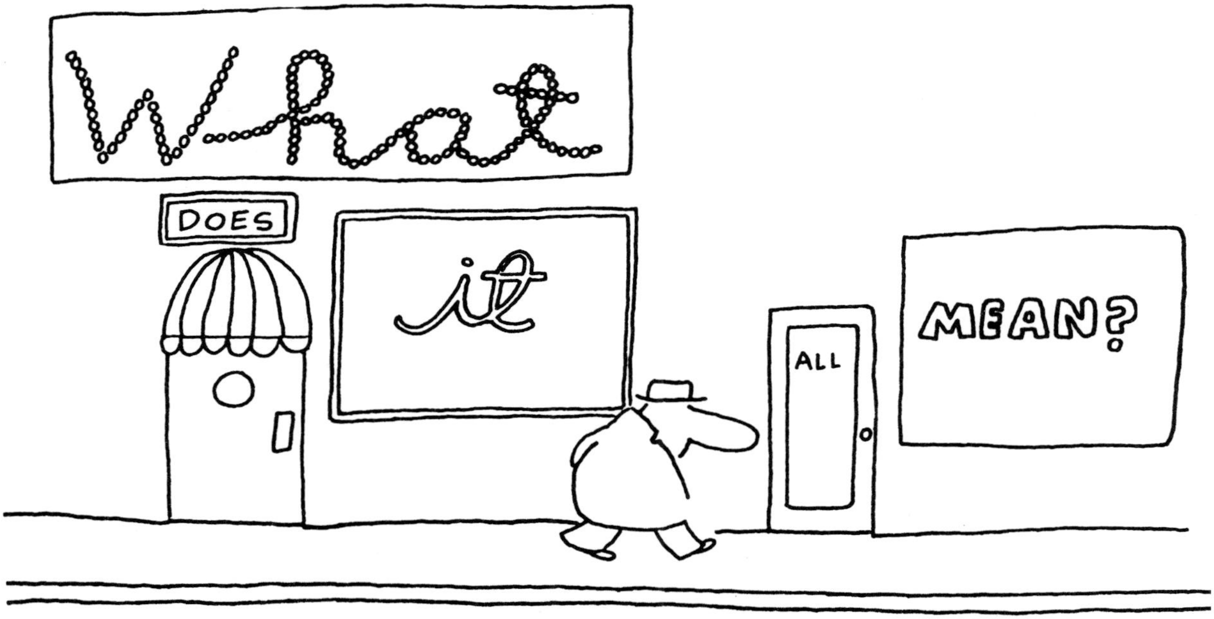
What
DOES
it
ALL
MEAN?

A BARSOTTI BIBLIOGRAPHY

COLLECTIONS OF CARTOONS BY CHARLES BARSOTTI

A GIRL NEEDS A LITTLE ACTION.
Harper & Row, 1969.

KINGS DON'T CARRY MONEY.
Dodd, Mead & Company
(paperback: Andrews & McMeel), 1981.

BARSOTTI'S TEXAS.
Texas Monthly Press, Inc., 1986.

THE USA TODAY CARTOON BOOK
(with Bruce Cochran and Dean Vietor).
Andrews & McMeel, 1986.

THE BEST OF C. BARSOTTI.
Rauette Books (U.K.), 1989.

SELECTED DRAWINGS BY CHARLES BARSOTTI

THE NEW YORKER 50TH
ANNIVERSARY ALBUM.
Viking Press, 1975.

THE NEW YORKER CARTOON ALBUM,
1975–1985.
Viking Press, 1985.

THE NEW YORKER BOOK OF COVERS.
Alfred A. Knopf, Inc., 1989.

Lee Lorenz, ed., THE ART OF
THE NEW YORKER.
Alfred A. Knopf, Inc., 1995.

BOOKS ILLUSTRATED BY CHARLES BARSOTTI

Martha Kaplan, THE NEW YORK
DOG OWNER'S GUIDE: EVERYTHING
YOU NEED TO KNOW ABOUT LIFE
IN THE CITY.
City & Co., 1994.

CHARLES BARSOTTI is a thirty-year contributor to *The New Yorker*. A compulsive doodler in his youth, his early inspirations came from the Sunday comics and the weekly magazines that his parents subscribed to, one of which—*The Saturday Evening Post*—published his first cartoons in the 1960s. In 1969, when the *Post* sank, Barsotti (along with George Booth) was hauled aboard *The New Yorker* by William Shawn. He has also written and illustrated books, created ad campaigns and comic strips, and worked for magazines as diverse as *Punch, Playboy, Barron's,* and *Texas Monthly*. Mr. Barsotti lives in Kansas City, Missouri, with his wife, Rae.

LEE LORENZ, an acclaimed cartoonist, was art editor of *The New Yorker* from 1973 through 1993. Mr. Lorenz and his family live in western Connecticut.